TENNIS COURSE

VOLUME 1

Techniques and Tactics

BARRON'S

TENNIS COURSE

VOLUME 1
Techniques and Tactics

English language edition published in 2000 by Barron's Educational Series, Inc.

Original title of the book in German is *Tennis Lehrplan, Bard 1: Technik & Taktik*

© 1995 BLV Verlagsgesellschaft GmbH, München/GERMANY

Tennis Course, Volumes 1 and 2
German Tennis Federation

Photo Credits
Baader: p. 8, 14 (right), 40, 96, 102, 108, 115, 120, 124, 134, 150
Birkner: p. 16 (bottom)
Bongarts: p. 2–3, 41, 70–71, 74, 92, 146
Exler: p. 15 (right), 16 (top), 22, 82, 86, 119, 130
Sutton: p. 23
Trotman: p. 126, 158
Zimmer: p. 10, 13, 14 (left), 15 (left), 17, 18, 25, 33, 37,
    42, 51, 52, 57, 76, 88, 100, 135, 162, 164, 168

ISBN: 0-7641-1485-9

Library of Congress Catalog Card No.: 99-069379

Translated from the German by Eric A. Bye, M.A.

Illustrations: Jörg Mair
Cover Photo: Duomo Photography/Chris Trotman
Cover Design: Network, Munich

Layout: Manfred Sinicki

BLV Publishing, Inc.
Munich Vienna Zurich
80797 Munich

All inquiries should be addressed to:
Barron's Educational Series, Inc.
250 Wireless Boulevard
Hauppauge, New York 11788
http://www.barronseduc.com

Printed in Hong Kong
9 8 7 6 5 4 3 2 1

Table of Contents

Introduction

The primary goal of this instructional book is to describe and explain the techniques of tennis as thoroughly as possible for the benefit of both teachers and learners. Explaining the techniques of tennis involves imparting an understanding of how to hit the ball, move around the court, and analyze and apply necessary moves. As a result, this manual contains a fairly comprehensive chapter about an elementary theory of movement. Additionally, individual elements of technique are treated in detail.

This attempt to provide the greatest possible insight into the interrelated skills involved in the technique of tennis has led to some intentional overlapping and repetition. We have assumed that instructional books are not generally read from beginning to end but are more likely to be used like a manual. That is, they should be consulted according to the reader's interest, need for instruction, and questions. Therefore, the repetition and overlapping are necessary for understanding some individual chapters.

It's important to know that developments in tennis technique are occurring every day. Also, in recent years, tennis instructors and experts have increasingly realized that individuality and personal style are crucial components to consider in tennis instruction. So, though the text that accompanies the illustrations describes how to perform the moves, considerable room exists for variation. In addition, world-championship players demonstrate how a personal style is founded on a mastery of basic techniques. Allowing for this latitude in instruction as a response to the learner's individual requirements makes teaching interesting but also difficult. It once again clearly demonstrates why a solid foundation is so important, which is that we've tried to offer in this book.

For reasons of simplicity and clarity, all descriptions of movements, including directions and sides of the body, are given from the viewpoint of a right-handed player. Lefties will have to transpose accordingly.

Volume 1, *Techniques and Tactics,* consists of two major sections. The first part presents fundamental theories of movement and the basic techniques. The second part deals with techniques used successfully in various situations where the learner is playing in different positions and with different purposes. Although we have attempted to present as much information as possible about theory and practice, we also realize that much is open to interpretation and discussion. We hope that this volume will be received enthusiastically, will be a valuable aid to many people, and will serve to stimulate further discussion.

Rüdiger Bornemann
Hartmus Gabler
Jock Reetz
Richard Schönborn

Basic Theory of Movement

The Concept of the Game

Observations about the theory of movement as a foundation for tactics and technique in tennis must be grounded in a clear understanding of the game. The observable characteristics of the game make sense only in light of that understanding.

The basic idea of tennis consists of using a racket to hit the ball out of your own court and over the net into your opponent's court.

Basic Tactics

In competitive tennis, the players' goals include the following:
- scoring points;
- causing the opponent to make mistakes; and
- avoiding mistakes,

with a view to winning games, sets, and matches. The rules provide for scoring points when opponents fail to reach a ball hit into their court or when they hit the ball into the net or out of bounds. The desired points can also be scored with the first hit. Often, however, many exchanges are needed to score a single point.

In *noncompetitive tennis,* players can operate within the general framework of the game but play in such a way that they avoid making mistakes and keep a rally going as long as possible. The process of rallying is therefore more important than the result.

In competitive tennis, players have many options in addressing their tactical goals. In order to score points, they can hit the ball in such a way that:
- the opponent fails to reach it in time and gives up a point;
- the opponent is made to run hard, or is put into a position where it's very difficult to hit the ball, thereby setting up a scoring situation or forcing the opponent to make a mistake; and
- the player avoids giving up a point.

In the course of a match, the player will also have to cope with a multitude of positions at the baseline, at midcourt, and at the net.

The Ball's Flight and Bounce

To use their resources in varied circumstances, players must take into consideration the behavior of a ball as it flies through the air and as it bounces on the surface of the court. The trajectory of the ball is determined by the following factors:
- the ball's flight direction (from down the line to crosscourt);
- the height of the ball's flight (from low to high);
- the ball's velocity (from slow to fast);
- the ball's rotation (topspin, backspin, or sidespin).

The way a ball behaves in a bounce is dependent upon the following:
- its velocity;
- its spin; and
- the angle at which it bounces.

In order to achieve the trajectory that corresponds to the tactical goal, the racket must be swung in a particular way up to the point where it makes contact with the ball. Specifically, this involves the following considerations:

- the speed of the racket head as it makes contact with the ball—this is a major determinant of the velocity of the outgoing ball;
- the direction of the shot with reference to space-related goals (such as crosscourt or down the line) and the stroke movement of the stroke with respect to the desired spin (topspin or backspin);
- the orientation of the racket face when it makes contact with the ball, since this affects the height and the placement of the shot.

Footwork

A ball that's hit by an opponent can land at an infinite number of spots on the court between the baseline and the net. This means that the player must get out of the starting position:

- early enough;
- quickly enough;
- with an economy of movement; and
- with adequate precision

to get to the ball quickly and return to a new ready position as expeditiously as possible. This movement to the ball and back into a new ready position is referred to as *footwork*.

Perfect footwork primarily presupposes an anticipation of the general direction and speed of the oncoming ball. It requires precise perception and fine-tuned footwork leading up to contact (hand-eye coordination) in order to hit the ball at the right distance from the body and precisely in the racket's sweet spot. Optimal footwork also requires great speed and coordination in the legs.

Precision and efficiency in footwork is a general requirement. Rapid decision making plus a quick and early start are important in situations that involve great time pressure (such as a return and net play) as well as with all fast, oncoming balls. All this makes footwork a crucial and performance-limiting factor in tennis.

Stroke Techniques

Once the player has assumed the optimal stroke position in a precise and timely fashion, completion of the tactical goal as previously described depends on imparting the correct speed and direction to the racket head.

The player must employ certain stroke techniques to accomplish the right effects with the racket. Technique is not a goal unto itself. However, if applied in a meaningful way, it facilitates the best of all possible moves with respect to the tactics demanded by any playing situation. Technique is also not a fixed quantity. Instead, its application must vary based on the context of a continually changing game; technique must be adapted accordingly.

Stroke technique primarily consists of contacting the ball in a precise manner and purposefully hitting it into the opponent's court.

In addition, the structure of the technique obviously depends on the player's individual circumstances and on a whole spectrum of external conditions.

The player's individual circumstances include the following:

- physical build, especially size, reach, and agility;

- abilities such as coordination, strength, endurance, and speed; and
- psychological factors such as motivation and intelligence.

The following external conditions also play a role:

- the behavior of an oncoming ball;
- the nature and composition of the court surface;
- the characteristics of the racket and how it is strung;
- the weather (for example, wind and sunshine); and
- the actions of the opponent(s) or partner(s).

In practice, a whole array of specific patterns have been developed within the framework of movement techniques. These are referred to as stroke techniques. Successful play comes from mastering these techniques and applying them to a variety of situations.

Coaches should be especially knowledgeable about stroke techniques and able to evaluate them. Coaches are in a position to instill these strokes in aspiring tennis players and to correct any errors that may crop up in their students' techniques.

At this point we will move onto a consideration of the theory behind footwork and stroke technique. After examining the behavior of the ball in flight and as it bounces, we will deal with basic tactics and stroke techniques.

Footwork in Tennis

Introduction

Tennis is one sport in which footwork is of paramount importance. There is no shot, including the serve, that escapes the profound influence of footwork for proper execution. Footwork, therefore, is almost unavoidably a performance-limiting factor.

Situations

On average, a tennis player hangs back about 15 feet (4 m) in a volley. The longest sprint is about 14 yards (14 m). The player may be required to run in any of these directions:

- sideways (parallel to the net)
- forward (straight or at a greater or lesser angle toward the net)
- backward (away from the net)

Stroke from a solid stance.

This involves running in curved as well as in straight lines. One example is when the player tries to anticipate the direction and the appropriate contact point of a serve and then gets back into position to cover the court effectively.

Situations arise where a player can make a shot from a solid stance and a good state of balance. However, many times hitting the ball from a full run, in a jump, from the wrong foot, or even while leaning back is either desirable or necessary. Good footwork is helpful in regaining balance in such situations. Players are balanced when their center of gravity is positioned over the support provided by both feet. The feet are at least shoulder width apart, the upper body is fairly straight, and the head is upright.

Jumping to make the shot.

Tasks and Goals

The purposes of footwork include the following:

- running to make contact with the ball in the most timely, appropriate, and economical manner;
- assuming an effective and well-balanced stance at the right distance from the most advantageous contact point with the ball;
- leading into and supporting the stroke; and
- running back to a favorable position on the court (in other words, covering the court effectively).

Coordination of footwork with the preparation and execution of stroke techniques is of paramount importance in tennis. While running, the player must start preparing for the stroke by twisting the upper body and taking the racket back to gain time before hitting the ball. The lead-in to the swing essentially begins with the legs. The coordination of the individual movements starts low and moves upward. This explains why a foot position that is stable and matched to the swing is a general prerequisite to achieving tactical goals.

The following sections describe the best ways to achieve desired results through footwork. However, footwork must remain flexible in accordance with individual characteristics and applicable situations and tasks.

Starting Stance

The term starting stance refers only to the time before the ball enters into play, as with *serves*

and *returns.* For a serve, the feet are in the starting stance in a solid position behind the baseline. Many players slightly shift their body weight back and forth to be better prepared for the serve. The distance between the feet and a more or less pronounced striding position can vary among individuals (see photos below).

On a return, the feet are usually in motion. This helps the player stay loose and poised for movement in this concentration phase for the transition to the readiness stance. The player may bounce back and forth or hop loosely in place on both feet. The player may also shift body weight fairly rhythmically from one leg to the other. The feet can be parallel to one another or in a striding position.

Ready Position/ Split Step

The ready position is used when the ball is in play. The player assumes this stance the instant the opponent hits the ball. The player bounces in a moderate straddling position (the ready position or split step, as in fig. 1). Feet are greater than shoulder width apart, body weight is distributed on the balls of the feet, and the ankles, knees, and hips are slightly flexed (fig. 2). This position allows the player to get a good start or continue running in any direction.

The legs should always be ready to run and in motion before assuming the readiness stance. On a return, the player often takes one or several steps to the front in order to use this movement in springing into the readiness stance.

The starting position in a serve varies among individual players.

Fig. 1 Jumping into the readiness stance.

Fig. 2 Posture in the readiness stance.

Stroke Position

It is common practice to make a distinction between a closed and an open stance. With forehand drives, the term *closed stance* is used when a line between the toes of both feet follows the precise direction of the ball's flight or angles to the right. If the line between the toes of both feet points to the left of the ball's direction of flight, the term *open stance* is used.

With backhand drives, the relationships are reversed.

With a closed stance, the toes of the foot closer to the net point more or less directly toward the net.

The open stance allows for better rotation of the upper body both in the backswing phase (windup) and the stroke phase (stroke dynamics).

In addition, when players are forced far out to the side of the court on the forehand side, they usually swing the racket from an open stance. That practice makes it easier for players to control their balance and to get into position more quickly for the next play.

The open stance is used primarily:
- on a return (forehand and backhand) and also when time is critical;

Open stance in forehand drive.

- with forehand ground strokes, especially when they must be played under pressure;
- with forehand topspin;
- with forehand topspin lobs;
- with a forehand slice attack; and
- with two-handed backhand shots

The lateral stroke position is used primarily:
- with a serve;
- with backhand shots;
- with volleys (forehand and backhand);
- with half volleys (forehand and backhand);
- with drop shots (forehand and backhand);
- with a slice-lob (forehand and backhand); and
- with forehand strokes, especially when accuracy is called for (for example, a passing shot when there's enough time available)

Open stance in two-handed backhand drive.

Support Leg (Anchor Leg/ Jumping Leg)

The leg that bears the body's weight as the racket is brought back in preparation for the swing is referred to as the support leg. In the case of right-handed players, this is:

- the left leg in a serve;
- the right leg in a forehand smash;
- usually the right leg in forehand drives (however, when the pressure is on, the player may spring off the left leg to get a fast ball);
- the left leg in a backhand volley;
- usually the right leg in backhand shots from a lateral position (with the toes pointing more or less to the front); and
- the left leg in backhand shots from an open stroke position.

In order to get into position to hit the ball, the player places the anchor leg the desired distance behind the anticipated contact point with the ball, usually heel first (except in the case of a serve or a smash). On dirt courts, players often slide with the anchor foot into the desired position (see photo below). In that case, the foot is planted on the entire sole or on the ball of the foot. If the player is using a forehand stroke in a closed position, the other leg is moved ahead toward the contact point *during* the shot to support the body weight and get back into balance. Here, too, the foot is planted heel first. With a backhand ground stroke

from a lateral position, the left leg supports the body weight at first. However, *before* the shot, the body weight shifts to the right leg (anchor leg). Balance is maintained by extending the anchor leg during the shot.

The anchor leg is referred to as the *jumping leg* when the player jumps off it to make a shot. This may occur during a smash from a jump and when the player has to jump to reach the ball in a good position with respect to height and distance (as in the volley pictured at top right).

Players also jump off their anchor leg in tight situations (for example, a backwards shot) and when dealing with fast attack shots. In such cases they also land on their jumping leg.

The term *support leg* is used when players use a separate step to check their horizontal motion and convert the movement into a more or less vertical direction by pushing off that leg. Examples occur during a jump smash and a forehand topspin shot.

Sliding in the stroke position.

A jump makes hitting the ball as a volley possible.

Running from the Ready Position to Various Positions on the Court

Running Sideways

Except in fairly long runs parallel to the baseline, the upper body should face toward the net.

Movement to the side begins using a side step with the leg that is closer to the contact point with the ball.

With very short distances of around 3 feet (1 m), this step is all a player needs to do to get into the stroke position. The foot and upper body are twisted toward the side where the ball will be hit. Therefore, it is also appropriate to refer to this as a *turning step*. For distances of 3 to 10 feet (1 to 3 m), the player starts with a side step and follows with a trailing step and then the twist step. The trailing step follows the side step very quickly. These three steps produce a typical cha-cha-cha running rhythm for baseline tennis.

Backhand swing from a forward run; the right foot points ahead diagonally toward the net.

In running to cover longer distances on the court, players start off using normal strides. The important thing is to start fast and reduce speed before assuming the stroke stance in order to contact the ball from a stable and well balanced position.

If enough time is available, the player can take several small steps before assuming the final stroke position in order to adjust to the anticipated flight and the contact point with the ball.

Running Straight Ahead

Running straight ahead is done using normal strides. With a forehand drive, the anchor leg is planted, the body is turned, and the foot is nearly parallel to the net. For a backhand drive, the anchor leg is placed in such a way that the foot points more toward the net (see photo above). The shot is made either on the run with an adjusting step or from a jump.

With a shot from a jump (usually to put pressure onto the opponent), takeoff and landing are done with the leg that is closer to the net.

Running Backward

Only in rare cases do players move back by running backwards. With a good lob, the player turns around and tries to sprint behind the anticipated contact point with the ball. In most other instances, the body is positioned sideways to the net. The player uses either side steps and adjusting steps or a crossover stride to move back. In a crossover stride, the leg closer to the net crosses *over* the other leg in order to maintain the sideways position.

Stopping Step/Starting Step

If the shot cannot be played from a solid position, the body moves in the original direction of motion *at the moment the ball is hit*. Then, after hitting the ball, the player takes another step in the same direction. This step should accomplish two things: it should check the player's movement (acting as a stopping step) and allow the player to push off from that leg (with a starting step) to cover the court.

With a stroke from an open stroke stance, this stopping and starting step is accomplished by effecting a small jump from anchor leg to anchor leg. With a stroke from a lateral or closed position, the player must make another small step in the original direction of travel. A quick start from the ready position is also done with a starting step in a direction opposite to the anticipated direction of run.

Running to an Advantagous Position on the Court After Hitting the Ball

After the player hits the ball, the dash to the next position on the court begins with a starting step (effectively a step in the wrong direction), is followed by a crossover step (directed toward the front), and concludes with side steps and adjusting steps. Normal running strides are used only to cover long distances after the starting step.

Stroke Techniques

Good footwork is a prerequisite for hitting the ball properly. Players must get into the best-possible position as quickly as possible relative to the oncoming ball in order to hit it and accomplish their tactical goal. In that regard, stroke technique involves swinging the racket in a manner that's appropriate for the flight and bounce of the oncoming ball and that addresses the player's tactical purpose.

In theory, how refined the stroke technique is may not matter much as long as the player succeeds in accomplishing the goal mentioned above. Just the same, as the game has progressed and top-level players and their coaches have striven to hit the ball and place it with greater speed and accuracy, specific

characteristics in stroke technique have evolved as a response to various situations. Individual refinements in stroke technique are an outgrowth of adjustments to concrete situational requirements and individual circumstances.

In the present tutorial, only the conventional stroke techniques will be included and described. Movements will also be analyzed in order to determine, at least in theory, the best possible way to perform them and to recommend that ideal as a point of reference for learners and coaches.

Footwork and stroke technique are well coordinated in this volley.

Theoretical Approaches to Movement Analysis

A number of ways can be used to analyze movement. They are distinguished from one another primarily by different perceptions and procedures on the part of the analyst.

Gohner formulates questions according to *how movements are performed,* their *order,* the *best way of executing them,* and their *purpose.* Distinguishing among methods involves proceeding in different ways: qualitatively (using subjective evaluation), quantitatively (with objective measurements), in a restricted or sports-specific context, or on a broader base.

The following special approaches are useful in examining the subject matter of this instructional:

- a biomechanical approach;
- a morphological approach; and
- a functional analytical approach

Biomechanical Approach

This approach is based primarily on the idea that in striving to achieve the best results, a maximum amount of mechanical work is applied against resistance. In addition, energy is used to its best advantage for specific types of movement (according to Hochmuth). This takes place under strict considerations of economy and the laws of mechanics as well as the build and the physiological functions of the human body. Universally applicable theoretical measurements have been formulated for all types of sports according to these conditions and corresponding demands for peak performance. These *biomechanical principles* allow one to assess all types of athletic movements qualitatively with a view to their greatest effectiveness.

Morphological Approach

The morphological approach, in contrast with the biomechanical approach, consists of describing outwardly visible characteristics and analyzing how a movement is performed from temporal, spatial, and dynamic viewpoints. Numerous experts from many types of sports were first asked to address the question of which observable characteristics constitute the most effective movement. These characteristics were recorded (by Meinel). They were supplemented by systematic observations and theoretical analyses of the goals and conditions associated with the corresponding movements.

The resulting *morphological characteristics of motion* make it possible to formulate a qualitative evaluation in three phases of how a movement is carried out.

Functional Analytic Approach

In his functional analytic approach, Gohner maintains that describing precisely how a movement is performed is not very useful in motion analysis. It's of much greater importance to know how the individual components of the movement are useful and how they help in accomplishing the goal of the movement. This therefore involves the *function of individual movements.* This function is a product of the movement's purpose and the surrounding conditions. The conditions that encourage or interfere with achieving the goal include the equipment, the environment, the rules, and the athletes themselves.

The functional analytical approach will be further explained in the following pages since it constitutes the basis for formulating the techniques in this instructional. It is a reasonable approach to do so because in tennis, technique is not a constant. As pointed out at the beginning, technique adapts to changeable external conditions and according to tactical goal setting. Even top-level players demonstrate different techniques in identical situations. Quite often these techniques appear to be totally different. A precise analysis clearly shows that certain parts of a movement are universal and that others are fundamentally different. Therefore, as a technique fulfills its function, some elements are apparently indispensable while others can vary within certain parameters. Questions arise as to what these elements look like, to what extent they may vary, and by what conditions they are determined. The answers come from the *functional analytical approach,* which is used in existing instructionals to describe and analyze technique. Based on their purpose and the conditions in which they are used, individual actions that constitute various techniques will be weighted differently, either as definite models or as ones that can be adapted within defined parameters. By way of background for these specific actions, this instructional will include a combination of the *biomechanical and morphological approaches* plus the normal behavior of a ball as it flies through the air and bounces off the surface of the court.

Biomechanical principles, morphological characteristics of movement, and physical and mechanical properties can be used to evaluate various actions in the newly identified structural phases that comprise various techniques.

The following pages will define the functional analytical approach in greater detail. Then this text will present in succession some morphological characteristics of movement, some biomechanical principles, and the physics of tennis balls in flight and as they bounce. This information will conclude with an explanation of the most important techniques.

The Concept of Functional Movement Analysis

Movement Goals

In the following sections, the functional analytical approach is referred to as the functional analysis of movement. A working understanding of movement is essential to this analysis. In other words:

- movements in tennis must always be understood as means to accomplishing tasks; they must be carried out in accordance with goals and within specific frameworks;
- goals and conditions are not conceived as constants, but are subject to change; and
- a tennis player's observable actions are usually dictated by goals to achieve and by prevailing conditions.

An example should make this clear. In serving, the primary task is to get the ball into play. In this case, a *possible solution* involves hitting the ball either from below or from above with minimal speed and without much spin. On the other hand, if the goal of the serve is to put pressure onto the opponent by hitting the ball fast and hard, the ball must be hit in such a way that it flies in a parabolic trajectory. All of this is affected by specific conditions such as the size and reach of the player, the height of the net, and the dimensions of the service court. Having

all this information allows one to deduce which of the player's actions are necessary, or at least fairly important, to achieving that goal.

The main idea of functional movement analysis involves determining which movements are appropriate to various goals and to existing conditions. It's also necessary to determine the functions of the player's actions with respect to the goals and conditions that are being analyzed.

Evidently, on the one hand some actions are so firmly established on biomechanical grounds that they can be considered as practically indispensable. On the other hand, some actions allow some latitude for variations.

In the first case, speaking of actions as either *right* or *wrong* is appropriate. However, in the second, categories such as *effective, less effective,* and *ineffective* are used.

Main Action

When using this approach, one may first inquire about goals and then take into consideration individual and material conditions. It is then possible to determine which of the player's actions are necessary and effective, take into account all conditions, and identify which supporting actions are absolutely necessary. A further example should make this clear. If a player intends to hit a ball at high speed from the baseline so that it bounces just in front of the opponent's baseline (consequently, a long shot), the desired goal can be achieved by the following actions:

- the player must accelerate the racket head up to the contact point to impart high speed to the ball;
- so the ball does not go too far and land out of bounds, the player should hit it with topspin; this will give it the right length, causing it to drop in flight and hit in front of the opponent's baseline; this forward spin is accomplished by swinging the racket so it hits the ball in a nearly vertical position and with a slight forward and upward motion; and
- the ball must be met at the right distance to the front and to side of the body in order to achieve two further goals: accuracy and safety.

This action—hitting the ball at high speed using a slight forward and upward motion with the racket in a nearly vertical position—is designated *the main action.* This main action is absolutely necessary in order to address the conditions that affect the goal. Figure 3 shows the stages of a forehand ground stroke. The stroke phase begins before the turning point of the curve and ends upon contact with the ball. The main action begins within the stroke stage along the lower part of the loop and likewise ends at contact with the ball. The structure of the racket's movement in the main action is precisely determined for any type of stroke technique. The speed and direction of the racket are determined by the momentary requirements of the game.

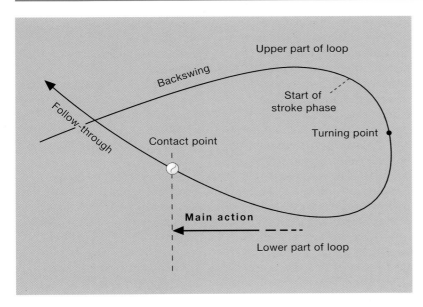

Fig. 3 Schematic representation of the loop described by a ground stroke.

Supporting Actions

A number of secondary actions also come into play in supporting the main action, but generally they are less rigidly prescribed:

- acceleration of the racket is best accomplished by using a fluid, arcing transition into the stroke phase; the form that this transition takes is not firmly fixed, though, since the desired acceleration can be accomplished without describing a pronounced curve;

- moving the forward leg in the direction of the stroke allows the player to place body weight onto the forward leg during the stroke phase; with a forehand ground stroke, the body is used to support the swing of the racket and to help direct the stroke; there's a lot of latitude in placing the leading leg and in determining how far apart the feet should be; those details depend on the required stability and on the actions that will follow the stroke (especially running);

- in imparting the desired speed to the ball, it's helpful to make contact at the right distance in front of and to the side of the body; in the case of a forehand ground stroke, the impact with the racket involves high resistance, and the ball rebounds with great force; some players use variations on the forehand grip that seem to serve the purpose well;

- continuing the swing through the stroke phase into the follow-through helps with control at the point of contact and improves the smoothness and economy of movement.

The following points describe some of the most important secondary actions that players can use to support the goal of imparting forward spin to the ball:

- bending the knees in the follow-through phase to make it easier to swing the racket forward and upward in the stroke phase;

- lowering the racket head at the start of the stroke phase so it can subsequently be swung upward and forward to meet the ball and create the desired topspin;

- straightening the legs in the stroke phase to support the stroke movement;

- using the forehand or backhand grip (in the case of a forehand or backhand ground stroke) so that the racket face is vertical at the instant it hits the ball at the best point in its trajectory;

- not all these supporting actions are absolutely necessary; nor is it always useful to prescribe such things as precisely how low the center of gravity should be, how far to lower the racket head, and how far to reach in a forehand stroke.

Possible Variations, Errors, and Flaws

On the basis of these explanations and by using movement analysis and correction, it's possible to formulate a preliminary answer to the question of what can be regarded as right and wrong in movements that are tailored to addressing tactical goals. The *main action* necessary to achieve a movement's purpose is clearly established. Any deviation from that established movement constitutes a defect. In the realm of *supporting actions*—especially in the backswing and follow-through stages and to a lesser extent in the stroke stage—there exists a lot of room for variation. Each action has its own accompanying advantages and disadvantages. It's quite difficult to specify the dividing lines among these variations.

In any case, an auxiliary action is faulty if it fails to support the main action effectively, interferes with it, or exerts any other negative influence on accomplishing the desired goal. Therefore, it's useful to think not only in terms of errors but also of flaws—even though the dividing line between flaws and errors is not always clear. This text considers flaws as those auxiliary actions that fail to provide optimal support for the main action. A flaw becomes an error when the disadvantages of the supporting action outweigh its advantages.

Style

Since supporting actions are subject to quite a number of variations, they allow for the greatest individual expression of movement, especially in the backswing and follow-through phases. These individual variations can be considered to constitute a player's *style of movement;* it is expressed primarily through the spatial and temporal structure of an entire motion. Characteristics of this individual dynamic and form include the range and rhythm of the movement. This applies especially to the serve, which often takes on very individualized characteristics, especially with respect to the length of the backswing and the timing of the acceleration into the main action.

These individual characteristics of movement depend, in turn, on a player's constitution, strength, speed, temperament, and motivation. This explains why players of smaller physical stature, for example, tend toward quicker movements and taller ones toward more deliberate and precise movements. Temperamental players prefer lively actions and fairly dramatic backswings. They tend to change their grip and use lots of different techniques. On the other hand, those who play a more defensive game prefer steadier, more economical, and more precise movements.

In tennis instruction, it becomes appropriate to recognize and make allowances for those types of individual personality traits, particularly because they contribute to the development of a personal style. If you watch world-class players in this light, an objective evaluation shows that while they possess consummate skills, they move in very different

An individualized style using a nearly straight arm in the backswing for a backhand slice.

ways. This leads to the conclusion that these players' main actions are practically perfect (and almost always effective) and that it's their supporting actions that express their personality traits in very individualized ways.

The Average Performance of a Movement

General Performance for Normal Situations

Up to this point, performances have been framed rather generally in terms of variations, errors, and flaws. The text has not yet considered such specific conditions of the target group as age, sex, size, and talent. It has also not examined specific situational conditions such as the court surface or the speed, trajectory, or bounce characteristics of the ball. Describing and developing the various stroke techniques must begin with normal situations and standard conditions. By this we mean a standard situation in which a ball is fed at average speed and with no heavy spin and where the other player can return the ball from an ideal contact point in front of and to one side of the body. Standard conditions refer to the learner's physical conditioning and coordination. If one were to film a great number of different learners as they function in a standard situation (a forehand ground stroke, for example) and superimpose the images so that they blend into a single movement, the result would be that movement's *standard* or *average performance*. This composite execution of a movement provides both an *average* and an *ideal* form relative to a standard situation. In reality, a multitude of situations and very individualized conditions come into play. As a result, variations in technique arise in response to different situations and personal circumstances. While an instructional text cannot address all the possible variations, the following two examples should help illustrate the point.

Variations in Technique: Special Solutions for Special Situations

Example 1: Top-Level Competitive Tennis

Due to the extreme demands of a match and the extraordinary abilities of the players, top-level tennis can entail significant deviations from standard ways of executing a movement. This can be briefly illustrated by Agassi's forehand topspin volley and Becker's blocked backhand return. In contrast with the recommendations commonly found in existing instructionals, which specify a "classical" forward and downward (slice) movement in a volley, Agassi often uses a forehand topspin volley. This is not imply that Agassi's delivery should be considered wrong according to the instructionals. Rather, the reader must take note of the situations and the conditions in which this ball is played. Agassi usually plays at the baseline. He moves forward only now and again, when he sees that his baseline shot can put a lot of pressure on the opponent. Consequently, the opponent can make only a relatively high and slow return without much power. Since the opponent starts running relatively late, he is forced to hit the ball at about midcourt. And since he has to hit the ball fairly high at midcourt,

Follow-through after a forehand topspin volley.

a normal volley would be too slow to be effective. This explains why Agassi plays (as in the photo on page 23) a topspin ground stroke with lots of momentum and forward spin. In so doing, he reduces the risk of hitting the ball less precisely and can simply apply his instinctive ground stroke and grip to a different situation.

As for Becker's blocked backhand return, this technique in this form is likewise nowhere to be found in the instruction books. It differs considerably from the average performance recommended for the backhand ground stroke. The deviation from the average performance of this stroke is attributable primarily to specific situational conditions and the player's individual capabilities. Becker usually plays this stroke when his opponent delivers a very fast serve on a fast surface and when he wants to return the ball as quickly as possible to deny the opponent a chance to come up close to the net. This is a combination of special situational conditions and a specific tactical goal. Becker performs this move from an open stance and without much backswing or body twist. He hits (blocks) the ball directly in front of his body by forcefully using his wrist to position the racket face vertically at the point of impact. Note that he can

successfully use this stroke only because he has exceptionally good reactions, great coordination, and the necessary muscular development.

The foregoing move is so far removed from "normal" tennis that it may never appear in any tennis instructional. (See also the photo on page 41.)

Agassi and Becker apply their particular moves in the best way possible from a functional and individual viewpoint.

Example 2: Children's Tennis

Children obviously have different physical characteristics than adults. For example, they are smaller and less powerful. These conditions have an effect on how children accomplish tennis-specific tasks. Children may have to perform these tasks differently than the instructionals dictate.

Because of their smaller body size, children may have to hit balls at shoulder height more frequently than adults do; that may involve a change to extreme forehand and backhand grips.

Due to their reduced arm strength, children tend to use both hands on a backhand shot. The second hand helps them to hit the backhand with greater control and speed. Using the two-handed backhand has practically no drawbacks because children are usually

very agile and are good at learning even bilateral motor skills.

These brief explanations show that the demands placed on children by playing on a full-size court necessarily differ from those experienced by adults. This clearly involves some fairly major departures from average stroke techniques. When children play using shorter rackets on a reduced court with slower flying balls that do not bounce as high, their techniques indeed approach the average normally described with reference to adults. With respect to long-term development of tennis technique, one might conclude that tennis for youngsters would be better if it were played under conditions that foster development of techniques similar to the ones they will need as adults (for example, by using lighter balls, shorter rackets, and reduced courts).

Both of the foregoing examples involve special (and to a certain extent individual) solutions in special situations. An instruction book designed to lay the groundwork for tennis cannot cover every possible situation in exhaustive detail. In part, such technical variations, especially at top levels of play, can be considered part of the latitude that individual techniques can encompass.

Adults as well as children must often hit a ball at shoulder height.

Qualitative Phenomena of Movement

Tennis-Specific Biomechanical Principles

The makeup of the human body and its functioning—that is, using the limbs in specific sequences by activating the muscles—constitute the biomechanical starting point for swinging the racket. The result is that sometimes the racket only approximates the ideal swing or follows it for only a short time. The most appropriate and effective biomechanical swing technique results from meaningful movements adapted to a given situation.

Biomechanical principles include mechanical laws of movement as applied to the human body. They serve to optimize technique with respect to specific conditions and the goals of a particular sport. The following tennis-specific principles are based on work by Hochmuth and Wiemann in the field of situational sports.

The Principle of the Best Opportunity to Hit the Ball

In any given situation, the ball has a particular speed, angle of flight, and spin. The chances of hitting it must be optimized in order to achieve precise placement in the opponent's field of play. In other words, the ball must be hit:

- precisely with the center of the racket;
- using the right grip;
- with the wrist held in an appropriate position;
- at the right distance to the side;
- in front of the body.

The trajectory of the ball essentially depends on the *precision* of the speed and the direction of the racket as well as on the *consistency* of the angle of the racket when it hits the ball.

The necessary precision in locating the contact point is a function of stroke technique, grip, and height at contact with the ball.

Placement precision is especially dependent on hitting the ball exactly in the center of the racket. Getting the body in exactly the right position with respect to the ball (offset to one side) and using careful hand-eye coordination make this precision possible.

The Principle of the Optimal Acceleration Path

To hit the ball at high speed, it's necessary to use an acceleration path that's as long as possible in combination with available muscle strength and coordination. The acceleration path should follow a straight or slightly curved line. The acceleration movement must be *fluid* and nearly perfect in regard to *extent* and *rhythm*. Increasing the precision of the stroke is as important as achieving high speed in the swing. A straight or slightly curved acceleration path oriented toward the goal necessarily produces greater precision in hitting the ball.

The Principle of Optimal Muscular Tension

To achieve a high terminal velocity in a swing, the muscles employed must be tensed as effectively as possible in the backswing motion. Tensing is accomplished by innervating the tensed muscles from bottom to top and from inside to out. Innervation merely consists of supplying a part of the body with nervous energy or nerve stimuli. Optimal tensing involves:

- tension that transfers smoothly and immediately into muscle contraction, whereby stored mechanical energy can be transformed into biochemical energy in the muscles (a rebound effect that increases the strength of the movement);
- tension that lies below the maximum possible level;
- tensing during the backswing phase in such a way that the tension progresses from bottom to top and from within to without so that it complements the individual movements that make up the swing (thereby coordinating the individual impulses).

Fig. 4 Winding up in the backswing phase of a topspin shot.

Fig. 5 Compensating movement in a backhand slice.

Fig. 6 Compensating movement in a jump smash.

The Principle of Coordinating Individual Impulses

To impart a high speed to the racket in the stroke phase, all contributing muscle groups must coordinate with one another to work in a sequence that moves from low to high and from within to without. That way the muscles can reach their optimal strength and contribute to acceleration at the point of contact with the ball. Therefore, not only do the arm and hand muscles move the racket, but the muscles in the legs and torso also greatly contribute to acceleration.

- The movement thus becomes more economical because the muscles of the arm and hand are supported.
- To increase the tempo of movement, the individual impulses mentioned above need to be interconnected as effectively as possible. Movement in the stroke phase must begin with the legs and proceed in succession through the adjoining body parts in an upward direction and from within to without. This amounts to a progressive transfer of impulses (impulse conservation). The speed of the next body part increases at the same time that the previous part slows down. This gives the racket its maximum speed as the last link in this chain, where all the individual impulses culminate.

The Principle of Compensating Movement

The law involving action and reaction (or effect and counter-effect) is applicable to the movement of the racket because of the particular qualities and specific requirements involved. This means that in the backswing phase, with a solid stance on the court surface, the best muscle tensing is accomplished by winding up the upper body with respect to the lower body. That allows the player to impart a greater speed to the racket head (see fig. 4).

In the stroke phase, there is an individualized compensating movement that comes from the left arm, the torso, and the legs, depending on the technique and the intended speed of the stroke. That movement helps control the shot (see fig. 5).

Also, in cases where the player is momentarily out of contact with the court surface during the stroke, the swing involves compensating movements (see fig. 6). These help with control and quick recovery of balance after landing.

Morphological Characteristics of Movement

With the help of the morphological characteristics of movement (see page 19), the composite qualities of various techniques can be assessed. Table 1 on page 28 presents this information.

Table 1 Morphological Characteristics of Movement (According to Meindel)

Basic Characteristics of Movement			Complex Characteristics of Movement		
	Movement	—Continuous flow of movement —Matching the strength of the impulse to external forces (Problems: changes in direction and timing of external forces)			
	Precision of Movement	—Coincidence of theoretical and actual values with respect to spatial, temporal, and dynamic characteristics —Accuracy in hitting the ball and addressing goals		Rhythm of Movement	—Characteristic temporal ordering of a movement, perceptible in dynamic, spatial, and temporal progression —Repetition of comparable fundamental elements
	Consistency of Movement	—Consistency among repeated movements			
	Scope of Movement	—Spatial extent of a movement in accordance with external conditions		Linking of Movements	—Connecting individual movements with respect to timing, extent, and exertion of force —Temporal displacement of individual movements and use of torso
	Tempo of Movement	—Speed of individual and composite movements with respect to external conditions			
	Intensity of Movement	—Amount of strength applied to the execution of a movement with respect to external conditions			

Developing Individual Elements of Technique

Tactical Qualities of Technique

As already explained, a player's actions in tennis are determined by the desire to score a point directly, to set up an eventual victory, or to wait for the opponent to make a mistake.

Observation of world-class players in action shows that even at that level of play, the majority of points come from errors made. This explains why tactics should first be directed toward avoiding mistakes. Returns must therefore *safely* reach the opposing court. Since the opponent will frequently take a calculated risk, tactics should also involve increasing the opponent's chances of making a mistake.

That can be accomplished only by improving one's *precision* and *variability* of play. In other words, the opponent should be forced out of the field of play and into difficult and hurried reactions by means of varied and very long shots and also by frequent changes in placement. Variation and an increase in *speed* must be governed by one's own risk tolerance, the height at which the ball is contacted, and one's position on the court. The speed and bounce of the ball can be influenced by varying its spin.

According to these observations, the essential tactical qualities in a tennis match consist of the following:

- reliability;
- precision; and
- speed.

For each playing situation, the ball has an ideal trajectory with respect to safety, precision, and speed. The nature of this trajectory is decided at the point of contact with the ball. The velocity and direction of the ball depend on the speed and direction in which the racket is swung and on the angle of the racket face at the instant of contact. The main action—the movement of the racket in the last part of the stroke phase, up to the point of contact, as well as the position of the racket at that moment—thus plays a major role in determining the nature of the shot.

That leads to the crucial question about how this desired main action can best be accomplished and what shape the backswing and stroke (auxiliary actions) must take to support the main action in the best possible way (see fig. 7).

The answer to this question must be based on biomechanical principles, morphological characteristics of movement (table 2), and laws of mechanics.

Accordingly, different goals must be addressed by different techniques and tactical qualities. Once these qualities have been ascertained, the aspiring tennis player can conceivably examine the corresponding techniques in the light of known biomechanical principles (see table 3).

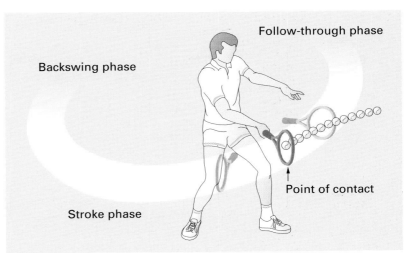

Fig. 7   Individual phases of a forehand stroke.

Table 2   Biomechanical Principles and Morphological Characteristics of Movement

Supporting Actions	Based on Biomechanical Principles	Morphological Characteristics of Movement
Main action	Best-possible chance to hit ball	Precision of movement Consistency of movement
Backswing and stroke phase	Best-possible acceleration path	Rhythm of movement Flow of movement Scope of movement
	Coordination of individual impulses (including impulse conservation)	Precision of movement Tempo of movement Force of movement
	Best-possible muscle tension	Linking of movements
	Compensating movement	
Follow-through phase	Compensating movement	Rhythm of movement Scope of movement

Table 3   Significance of Biomechanical Principles for Tactical Qualities

Tactical Qualities	Biomechanical Principles
Safety	Best-possible chance to hit ball
Precision	Best-possible chance to hit ball
	Best-possible acceleration path
	Compensating movement
Speed (achieved through use of acceleration paths)	Best-possible acceleration path
Speed (achieved through use of acceleration forces)	Coordination of individual impulses
	Best-possible muscular preliminary tensing
	Compensating movement

Hitting the Ball

As explained earlier, the desired trajectory of the ball is a function of the speed and direction in which the racket is swung, the position of the racket face, and hitting the ball at the best possible point.

Position of the Racket Face

For practically all shots, the racket face should be held essentially vertical.

That way, directing the shot and precisely placing the ball are a product of the speed and the direction in which the racket is swung. Varying the angle of the racket face provides additional control and constitutes yet another factor with which to contend. In practice, one can observe minor deviations from a vertical position of the racket face, especially when the ball is hit at various heights (Gabler and Gohner).

As an example, a deep slice may involve a variation of about 15 degrees in the attitude of the racket face. Just the same, the *usual recommendation* of a vertical position of the racket face, combined with a firm wrist at the moment of contact, remains valid. The term *firm wrist* has implications for the angle between the back of the hand and the forearm. This depends on the direction of the stroke (down the line or crosscourt) and is a result of the position of the long axis of the racket at the instant of contact with the ball. Page 34 provides further information about proper grip.

Wrist Action in Tennis

Based on a biomechanical chain reaction (or a coordination of individual impulses), the last part of the stroke movement concentrates all the energy of the entire body's movement in the forearm so that the energy can ultimately be released or discharged. The object is to produce a sharply increasing velocity in the racket in the final part of the swing movement.

The primary source of this is a rotation that involves using the muscles of the torso. The wrist, where a forcible stretching takes place in the rotators, acts as the link between the racket and the forearm. It consciously or unconsciously comes into play (as in a serve or a baseline shot) in the last part of the stroke movement. That happens in the following way. In the first part of the stroke movement, where the racket is swung in a rearward or a lower arc, when executing a baseline shot or a serve, respectively, dorsal flexion or stretching occurs in a forehand shot and a serve (see fig. 8). With a backhand shot, palmar flexion or bending occurs (as in fig. 9).

As the racket moves rearward, the forearm is already accelerating in the direction of the stroke. Since the player grips the racket relatively loosely at this point, the wrist muscles are relaxed. As a result, in a forehand shot, the wrist opens up or stretches, and in a backhand shot, it closes or bends (dorsal and palmar flexion). High terminal velocity in the stroke is thus achieved when there is plenty of inertial resistance and the forearm muscles are put into play at the last moment.

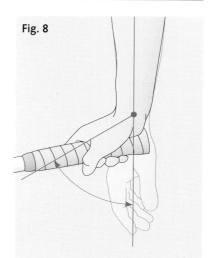

Fig. 8

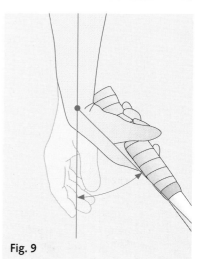

Fig. 9

Fig. 10

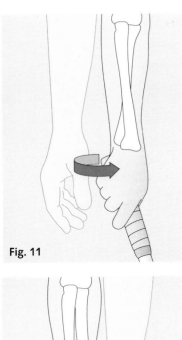

Fig. 11

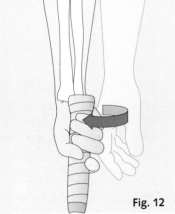

Fig. 12

Fig. 13

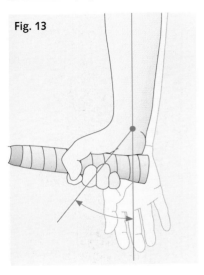

In the next part of the stroke movement, the forearm is drawn inward by the wrist. This transfers the impulse from this last link in the chain reaction to the racket.

During the stroke movement, ulnar flexion also occurs. In other words, the hand moves in the direction of the little finger. This is a product of shortening the ulnar flexor, as depicted in figure 10.

This relatively long muscle (about 8 inches [20 cm]) can contract very quickly. Doing so allows this muscle to take over the active acceleration task in this phase of the stroke movement. The ulnar flexor thus plays a significant role in accelerating the racket; the timing and the force of this acceleration vary according to the stroke used.

Further issues include pronation (that is, turning the forearm inward, as in fig. 11) in the serve and in forehand shots and also supination (turning the forearm outward) in backhand shots (fig. 12). These actions help to determine the direction of the shot.

Ulnar flexion continues at the contact point in a serve. With a forehand topspin and a backhand topspin shot, on the other hand, a radial flexion occurs. Radial flexion involves moving the hand in the direction of the thumb, as depicted in figure 13.

To summarize, as the racket speed increases up to the point of contact with the ball, the wrist performs three or four distinct movements in conjunction with the forearm. All of this takes place in a tenth or a hundredth of a second.

The wrist is held firm at the contact point for just about three- to five-thousandths of a second. In that brief instant, the wrist must provide some resistance to the ball. In the process, the forearm muscles are strongly innervated for a moment through the hand's firm grip on the racket. At that time, the wrist must be in its natural midrange—neither arched not bent. The position of the wrist must also be coordinated with the intended direction of the ball.

The so-called snapping of the wrist (palmar flexion), which people formerly thought was a function of the wrist at the contact point, is not used in hitting the ball. Only in the last phase of the follow-through can the wrist snap over in certain strokes (such as in service). This is a product of relaxing the forearm muscles and of the weight of the racket. This exerts no further influence on the ball, though, and is merely an economical conclusion to the entire stroke.

The Best Distance from the Body for Hitting the Ball

The contact point for all shots (except overhead) should be in front of the body and offset a comfortable distance to the side. Essentially, that provides a longer acceleration path for the racket and better opportunities to hit the ball.

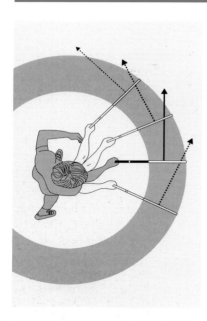

Fig. 14 (left) Optimal contact for a shot down the line.

Fig. 15 (right) Movement of the racket axis, particularly the racket head. The time interval between positions amounts to about 4/1,000 of a second. The illustrated scale yields the following data. The speed of the racket (measured at the outside point of the racket head) right before the contact point approaches 50 miles (80 km) an hour. Immediately after contact, the racket is moving at just over 20 miles (35 km) per hour. The ball, which is not illustrated here, is traveling at a speed of about 15 miles (25 km) an hour before contact and 56 miles (92 km) an hour after contact.

Precision in contacting the ball is achieved by adjusting the speed of the racket with respect to the velocity of the oncoming ball. Deviating from the optimal contact point is an obstacle to placing the shot precisely (see fig. 14). As figure 15 shows, the racket swings in an arc up to the contact point, momentarily moves at a right angle to the trajectory of the ball as a result of making contact with it, and then resumes its movement in an arc. This means that optimal contact with the ball is even more important than previously believed.

Just the same, the previously recognized requirement of following a contact line after a long stroke movement in the direction of the shot makes sense. It empirically leads to greater precision of contact with the ball and firmness in the wrist—especially when combined with the following:
- *forceful upper body rotation* in forehand shots, serves, and smashes;
- a degree of relaxation in the upper body in backhand shots; and
- a weight shift in all shots.

The appropriate *distance to the side* is reached basically by bending the elbow in a forehand shot (fig. 16) and by straightening it in a backhand shot (fig. 17). The *contact height* naturally depends on the ball's trajectory and the way it behaves in a bounce. The theoretical best contact height for a baseline shot is about hip level. However, the play situation frequently presents a *different contact height*:
- high bouncing topspin balls inevitably produce contact heights over shoulder height;
- most volley shots involve a contact point over hip height;
- low bouncing slice balls offer low contact points at knee level or below (see photo on p. 33).

Fig. 16 Side distance from ball in a forehand baseline shot (arm bent).

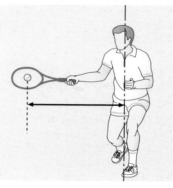

Fig. 17 Side distance from ball in backhand baseline shot (straight arm).

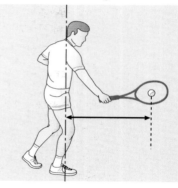

Problems with Shots from a High Contact Point

- The shorter lever between the rotational axis of the shoulder and the racket hand basically demands a greater expenditure of energy. The problem is mitigated, though, if the player can respond by hitting topspin and by accelerating upward from an advantageous, lower turning point in the stroke to create a longer lever.
- Some types of grip are unsuited for hitting the ball in front of the body.
- The follow-through must be adapted to the situation.

Problems with Shots from a Low Contact Point

- In order to avoid hitting the ball out of bounds, the stroke speed should remain low when responding with a straight shot.
- To reduce net errors, it may be necessary to adjust the position of the racket face by twisting the forearm when responding with a straight shot; responding with a slice works better since the ball rises as a result of the backward spin.
- Topspin shots from a low contact point are usually harder to hit than ones from a higher contact point since in the former case only a flat lower arc is possible, and that allows hardly any room for accelerating in an upward motion.
- Just before hitting the ball, the player must lower the center of gravity.

With *serves and smashes*, the location of the contact point is determined not only by the need for a long acceleration path but also by the function of the racket as the last link in a kinetic chain and the use of maximum reach. As a result, the following contact points are possible:

Contact Point with a Straight Serve:

- 4 to 12 inches (10–30 cm) in front of the left foot in the desired direction;
- at maximum contact height.

Contact Point in a Serve with Spin:

- slightly left (twist) or right (slice) of the anticipated direction;
- over the head, up to 8 inches (20 cm) in front of the left; foot in the desired direction
- leg twist below the maximum contact height.

Contact Point in a Smash:

- slightly in front of the head;
- at maximum contact height.

The Significance of Grip for the Shot

The grip, or the position of the hand on the handle of the racket, is an essential ingredient in hitting the ball most effectively.

The best grip affords a favorable contact point in front of the leading hip plus the essential vertical positioning of the racket face. This optimizes the transfer of force.

In the following paragraphs we will describe typical grips as they are seen in championship tennis.

That some rather fluid lines separate similar grips will be evident. The recommended grip for each shot (see table 4) contributes to the effective positioning of the racket face at the best contact point; an unfavorable or faulty grip makes that more difficult or impossible.

The illustrations of the grips show the hand positions at the contact point.

Forehand Grip (Eastern Grip)

When the racket face is held vertically, the hand grasps the racket handle from the right in such a way that the ball of the little finger lies on the rear of the right broad facet of the grip (see fig. 18).

Recommended For:

- shots on the forehand side, especially for contact points at hip height and slightly higher.

Inappropriate or Ineffective For:

- backhand shots;
- serves and smashes.

Extreme Forehand Grip (Western Grip)

As the racket face is held vertically, the hand holds the grip at an angle from below right in such a way that the ball of the little finger lies on the lower right bevel of the grip (see fig. 19).

Recommended For:
- topspin on the forehand, especially for contact points considerably above hip height; and
- topspin lob on the forehand.

Acceptable For:
- ground stroke on the forehand; and
- half volley on the forehand.

Inappropriate and Ineffective For:
- slice on the forehand (including slice lob);
- volley on the forehand;
- shots on the backhand side; and
- serves and smashes.

Semicontinental Grip

With the racket face held vertically, the hand grasps the handle at an angle from above right. The ball of the little finger lies on the upper-right bevel of the grip (see fig. 20).

Acceptable For:
- baseline shots on the forehand; however, not usable for contact points in front of the body without opening up the wrist and straightening the elbow;
- ground strokes on the backhand; turning the forearm (supination) is necessary with an early contact point;
- volleys on the forehand and backhand (with appropriate turning of the forearm);
- slice on the forehand and on the backhand (with appropriate turning of the forearm);
- service and smashes; and
- lob and drop shots.

Ineffective For:
- relatively high contact points; in order to keep the contact

point in front of the body, the forearm must be turned rather forcefully to keep the racket face in a vertical position.

Backhand Grip (Continental Grip)

The hand grasps the racket from above as the racket face is held vertically (see fig. 21). The ball of the little finger lies on the upper small bevel of the handle. A variation on this, the extreme backhand grip, involves placing the ball of the little finger onto the left upper bevel of the handle (see fig. 22).

Recommended For:
- all shots on the backhand side; and
- serves and smashes.

Inappropriate and Ineffective For:
- all forehand shots.

Two-Handed Backhand Grip

The right hand grasps the handle from the side, as with the forehand (and sometimes from above, as with the backhand grip), and is placed at the end of the handle. The left hand is located immediately in front of the right and grasps the handle from the left, as with a left-handed player's forehand grip (see fig. 23).

Use of the left hand permits an especially good transfer of force, depending on the direction of the shot, since the hand is positioned behind the racket handle. That arrangement also facilitates greater acceleration.

Since the left hand supplies the force for the stroke and the right hand is used primarily to provide stability, the left needs to be well trained in this movement.

Recommended For:
- ground strokes on the backhand; and
- topspin on the backhand.

Backswing Phase

The backswing phase serves to set up an optimal acceleration path with regard to length and direction.

The take back begins with a twist in the upper body. At the end of the backswing, there is a hesitation in the movement of the racket head that permits an accumulation of energy.

The backswing movement is ultimately influenced by:
- the amount of time available
- the tactical goal and type of shot; and
- individual circumstances.

Backswing with Baseline Shots

A backswing in a rearward and upward direction assures:
- use of the potential energy in the mass of the racket; and
- a fluid transition to the stroke phase.

The time available for a backswing is from a second to a second-and-a-half in a baseline duel and, in extreme cases, about four-tenths of a second in a return. Since about six- to nine-tenths of a second are needed for the bow-shaped backswing and stroke movements, the take back can be shortened only in returning fast

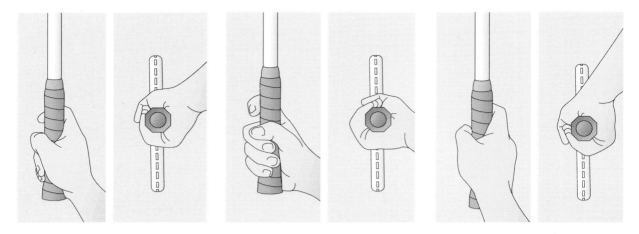

Fig. 18 Forehand grip seen from above and behind.

Fig. 19 Extreme forehand grip seen from above and behind.

Fig. 20 Semicontinental grip for forehand from above and behind.

serves. The start of the backswing depends on the velocity of the oncoming ball and the anticipated stroke technique. The take back must occur earlier in a slice since the entire movement is slower than with topspin shots. The backswing can take different forms. A fairly broad, rising arc makes it easier to accelerate the racket before the turning point in the loop. However, if the arc is too great, it may become harder to hit fast balls soon enough.

Straight-line take backs complicate racket acceleration and timing since before the forward swing occurs, the racket has to be stopped and then accelerated anew.

An analysis of world-class tennis shows that backswing movements of various players in similar situations can differ greatly (see fig. 24 and 25). However, these movements remain practically unchanged when the same player deals with varying situations involving different backswing and stroke speeds. The various movements evidently are a product of how the players learned the game and developed their individual styles. The variations originate from different sources rather than from the same movements in hand, elbow (or forearm), and shoulder (upper arm and torso). The backswing phase can be lengthened or shortened according to the demands of

the situation. Lengthening the backswing can be accomplished by:

- turning the upper body toward the rear;
- loosely straightening the elbow (with a forehand shot) or keeping the forearm close to the torso (with a backhand);
- bending the knees; or
- opening or closing the wrist (straightening in a forehand or bending in a backhand); the opening or closing of the wrist is more pronounced due to the centrifugal force of rapid backswing movements; with slower strokes, avoid conscious or extreme opening and closing of the wrist.

Table 4 Appropriate Grips for the Most Important Shots

	Baseline Shot	Topspin	Slice	Volley	Smash	Service
Forehand Side	Forehand grip	Extreme forehand grip	Forehand grip, semicontinental grip	Forehand grip, semicontinental grip	Backhand grip, semicontinental grip	Backhand grip, semicontinental grip
Backhand Side	Backhand grip, two-handed backhand grip	(Extreme) backhand grip, two-handed backhand grip	Backhand grip, semicontinental grip	Backhand grip, semicontinental grip	Backhand grip, semicontinental grip

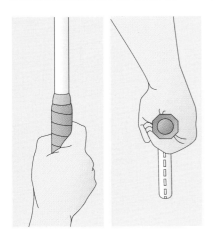

Fig. 21 Backhand grip seen from above and behind.

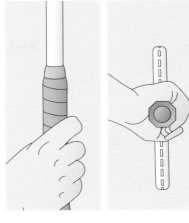

Fig. 22 Extreme backhand grip seen from above and behind.

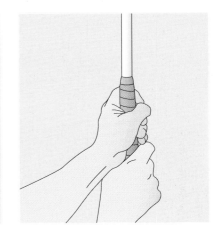

Fig. 23 Two-handed backhand grip seen from above; right hand using backhand grip.

Fig. 24   Fairly flat backswing in a forehand ground stroke from the baseline.

Backswing for Volleys and Half Volleys

Since the available time for a volley is often less than six- to nine-tenths of a second, the racket should be taken back by turning the shoulder only slightly to the rear. It must be raised above the anticipated contact height, for the volley shot is generally hit with back-spin (see "Stroke Phase"). The form of a take back for a half volley approximates the movements used for a ground stroke. However, because of the time pressure mentioned above, the take back movement has to be flatter and shorter.

Backswing for Service and Smash Shots

In a serve and a smash, using a long lever comprised of the arm and the racket while holding the racket high above the shoulder affords a good rhythm for the shot and helps the player maintain necessary balance. A long acceleration path is set up in the backswing phase of the service by means of:

- optimal movement downward and behind the back (which helps with acceleration);
- opening the wrist due to centrifugal force;
- bending the upper body far to the rear; and
- bending the knees.

Stroke Phase

Stroke Phase with Shots from the Baseline

The stroke phase begins by accelerating the racket before the turning point in the curve (see p. 21). In order to achieve a nearly straight or slightly curved acceleration path, the racket must be positioned as early as possible below or above (for topspin and backspin, respectively) the antici-pated contact point with the ball.

Good coordination among individual movements is essential for hitting the ball precisely and for running and hitting efficiently. When the shot requires extreme precision and speed at the same time, the individual movements must be in exact temporal and dynamic harmony to deliver maximum power. This is particularly the case with topspin balls. The coordinated body parts consti-tute a kinetic chain, or a system of component parts, that are linked together. Muscles serve to move the limbs and flex the joints. The possible movements of the body begin with the torso and move outward. That means that coordinating straight-line movements in the most distant extremities is difficult; but at the same time, a whiplike effect makes it possible to achieve greater speeds. This occurs because the racket is the last link in the chain and has the greatest moment of inertia. As the upper arm accelerates, the racket at first lags behind

Fig. 25 Very high backswing for a forehand ground stroke from the baseline.

momentarily. Pausing in the upper arm movement (braking) speeds up the racket considerably and swings it forward. Developing an effective transfer of movement means beginning the stroke movement in the legs and passing it through the torso, the arm, and the hand. Note that the spatial, temporal, and dynamic unfolding of the stroke movement must be planned early since no corrections can be made in the last part of the forward swing.

In addition, the speed of the racket head can be significantly increased by further bending the elbow. The bending reduces the radius and the moment of inertia, thereby increasing angular velocity.

Stroke Phase for Volleys

With a tennis ball traveling at high velocity and the attendant exaggerated bouncing characteristics that are often encountered in volley situations, a stroke movement in a forward and downward direction can be used to create backspin. The main factors in this are:

- the desired distance imparted to the ball can be achieved even at lower racket speeds; and
- the ball bounces off the surface low and therefore advantageously from a tactical standpoint.

This volley shot, which has been hit with backspin, also has the advantage that the movement can be performed in a more restrained and controlled manner. That is helpful with lower contact points. Additionally, coordination is better between the arm swing and the forward and backward movement of the body since both movements can complement one another with respect to direction and acceleration. It's easier to hit the ball as it rises since the downward direction of the stroke follows the approximate trajectory of the oncoming ball.

Stroke Phase in Service and Smash Shots

With serves and smashes, the movement of the racket should produce safety, accuracy, and a very high ball velocity. Therefore, the best possible coordination of the individual movements is of the utmost importance. *The stroke phase must originate from a straightening of the ankles and the knees.* Contractions in the muscles of the loins, abdomen, chest, shoulder, arm, and hand must follow in immediate succession. Coordinating a whiplike movement in the kinetic chain by straightening the ankles and knees produces a subsequent pushing off from the court surface. The wrist is still open, and the elbow is increasingly bent at this point in the arc (see fig. 26). The arc is most effective when the muscles involved in the stroke are not tensed to the maximum at the lowest point and the stroke hand is located

Fig. 26 Coordination of leg and arm work in a serve.

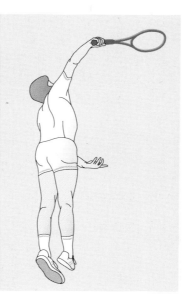

Fig. 27 Pronation movement and freedom of stroke side in a serve.

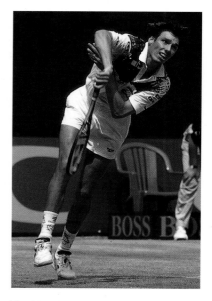

Fig. 28 Compensating movement from the throwing arm in a serve.

behind the head and slightly higher than neck level.

In order to present the racket face at a right angle to the flight direction of the ball, the forearm must execute a pronation movement in the stroke phase by turning the thumb side in. This is clearly continued into the follow-through phase (see fig. 27).

Throughout the stroke phase, the stroke shoulder of the racket arm is positioned nearly vertically over the left foot, and the axis of the shoulder is pointed high overhead. The freedom of the stroke side (see fig. 27) allows the kinetic chain to work vertically and in a straight line

to produce the best possible whiplike effect in accelerating the racket.

This also makes it possible to achieve the maximum contact height with the ball. The more forcefully the legs are straightened, the quicker the takeoff from the court surface (see fig. 28).

The left arm, which reaches upward with the ball, is lowered at the start of the stroke phase and must be angled across the upper body as the stroke is carried out (see fig. 28). This compensating movement is necessary to maintain control during the stroke.

Follow-through Phase

The optimal stroke rhythm facilitates a gradual reduction in speed toward the end of the movement. The stroke movement must be economical. Otherwise, slowing down the racket will consume energy.

The follow-through phase can help with control of the preceding hit. With hard-bouncing shots such as volleys and returns, it may help to block the follow-through by tensing the muscles into a solid resisting force (as in the photo on p. 41).

Blocking the follow-through on a return.

The Ball in Flight and Bounce

Tactical considerations on the one hand and technical developments on the other are influenced by the behavior of the ball as it flies through the air and bounces on the surface of the court.

The following explains how the stroke movement acts on the ball and on the ball's trajectory, and how the ball behaves in a bounce. At the outset, this presentation does not mention that the ball to be hit already possesses a particular velocity, direction, and spin. These considerations will be treated in the concluding paragraph.

Factors Affecting the Ball's Trajectory and Bounce

The following criteria determine the trajectory of a ball:
- its flight speed (fast or slow);
- its direction of flight (high, level, right, or left);
- its spin (forward, backward, or to the side);
- its wind resistance; and
- gravity.

Bounce characteristics are a product of:
- the ball's velocity at contact with the surface of the court;
- the angle at which it bounces onto the court surface;
- the ball's spin; and
- the makeup of the surface (cinders, synthetics, grass, and so forth).

Contact Between Racket and Ball— Effect on the Ball's Trajectory

The Nature of a Hit

The racket is purposefully swung against the oncoming ball. Hitting the ball with the racket is an impact event produced by complex swinging processes involving the racket and the arm. When the speed of the racket is tranferred to the ball, the ball is momentarily distorted and compressed as a function of its elasticity.

The higher the speed of the racket, the greater the distortion of the ball. The ball accelerates due to the speed of the racket and the resolution of its distortion. Two fundamentally different possibilities can happen when hitting the ball with the racket:

Table 5   Key to Subsequent Illustrations

S: Midpoint of ball
V_s: Racket speed
V_B: Speed of ball after contact
V_1: Speed of ball before bouncing onto court surface
V_2: Speed of ball after bouncing off court surface
a: Distance of stroke impulse from ball's center of gravity
u: Rotation speed (spin) of ball after contact
u_1: Rotation speed of ball before bouncing onto court surface
u_2: Rotation speed of ball after bouncing off court surface
α: Angle of contact (angle of descent) between ball and either racket or court surface (side view)
β: Angle of departure (thrust angle) of ball from racket or court surface (side view)
P: Impulse
Px: Horizontal portion of impulse
Py: Vertical portion of impulse
Q: Diagonal (Magnus) force on the rotating ball
L: Relative air currents

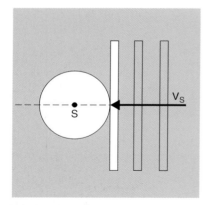

Fig. 29   Central contact.

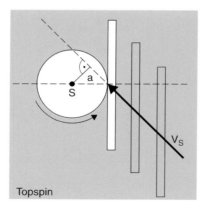

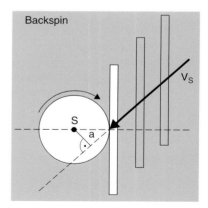

Fig. 30   Possibilities in hitting off center.

- On the one hand, the racket hits the ball directly on center; that is, the striking impulse (mass of racket × racket speed) is directed at the ball's center of gravity S (see fig. 29).

  A large portion of the racket's energy converts to energy of motion in the ball, which picks up essentially no spin.

- In the second scenario, the racket hits the ball off center; that is, the striking impulse is no longer directed at the ball's center of gravity S (see fig. 30). One part of this impulse is converted to flight impulse in the ball, and another part becomes a turning impulse that causes the ball to spin around its center.

While the vertical portion of the racket's speed (V_{s_y}) as it encounters the ball determines the amount of spin, the ball's velocity is a function of the horizontal portion (V_{s_x}) (see fig. 31).

With equal racket speeds in the stroke phase, the spin increases and the velocity of the ball decreases as the racket is swung upward at a greater angle.

Usually, the V_{s_x} speed portion is greater than the V_{s_y} portion.

The Ball's Flight Speed

Flight speed is a product of the following factors that come into play at the moment of contact between the ball and the racket:
- racket speed;
- distance between the direction of force and the ball's center of gravity (direction of racket movement; see fig. 30);
- speed of the oncoming ball; and
- elasticity of the racket, the strings, and the ball.

Thus, the velocity of a ball that's been hit is essentially controllable through the speed and direction of the racket as it swings forward. This is predicated on a firm grip at the instant of contact and on hitting the ball with the best part of the racket's face (see fig. 32). Otherwise, velocity and precision will suffer. This optimal contact point (the sweet spot) is not necessarily the same as the geometric center of the racket face.

The Ball's Departure Direction

Departure direction is designated by the angle of flight with respect to the level court surface (see fig. 33) and the sideline (see fig. 34). It is a product of the following factors:
- the racket's direction of movement (upward or downward, right or left);
- the racket's angle of inclination at the moment of contact; and
- the speed, the direction, and the spin of the oncoming ball.

Ball with No Spin

The racket is swung directly against the ball (see fig. 29). The direction of the striking force thus points precisely at the ball's center of gravity. The ball leaves the racket face at a right angle. The ball's trajectory describes a ballistic curve. It deviates from an ideal parabola because of wind resistance. The trajectory is shorter, and the angle of drop is somewhat steeper than the takeoff angle (see fig. 35). Observation of players in action shows that the majority of balls are hit at about hip or net level.

For a ball with no spin to clear the net when it's hit at this height, the racket face must be slightly open (see fig. 35). The takeoff angle is a function of the distance the ball has to travel and a departure speed tailored to the requirements of the situation:

- At any given speed, a departure angle of about 45 degrees will produce the longest flight distance and the most economical expenditure of energy. At that angle, the ball should reach the baseline even with lower racket speeds and fairly safe heights over the net.
- Departure angles greater or less than 45 degrees shorten the flight distance.
- The faster the racket is swung, the greater the ball's flight distance. This increases the risk of hitting the ball out-of-bounds.
- As the takeoff angle decreases and the ball clears the net at a lesser height, the racket speed must be increased to produce the same effect (making the ball reach the baseline). That increases the risk of a net fault.

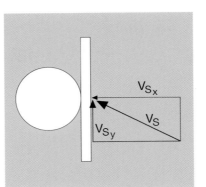

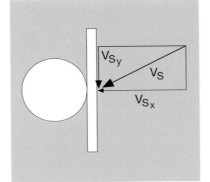

Fig. 31 Parallelogram of forces on a ball hit off center.

Fig. 32 The best contact point or sweet spot.

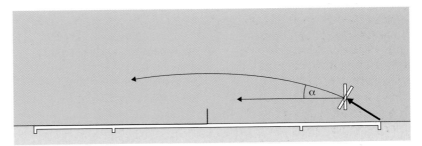

Fig. 33 Possible departure angles (high and low).

Fig. 34 Possible departure angles (right and left).

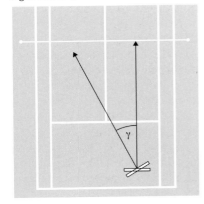

Fig. 35 Flight curve of a ball with no spin.

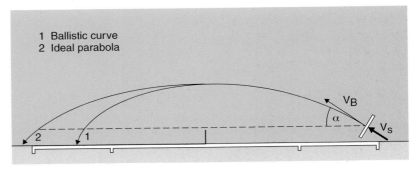

1 Ballistic curve
2 Ideal parabola

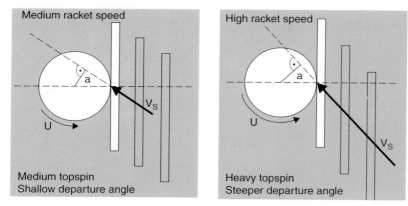

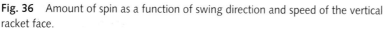

Fig. 36 Amount of spin as a function of swing direction and speed of the vertical racket face.

Ball with Topspin

The racket is swung against the ball from behind and below in an upward and forward direction. The racket face must remain vertical upon impact. The impulse of the hit thus points not at the center of the ball, but rather, above it. That is how the ball picks up topspin in addition to its departure velocity. The amount of topspin depends on the speed and direction of the racket swing (upward at a greater or lesser angle; see fig. 36).

Effect of Topspin on the Ball's Trajectory

As a result of topspin, air is carried along by the felt of the ball. During the flight topspin creates a layer of air that rotates with the ball (see fig. 37). This circulating current overlaps with the currents in the surrounding air (wind resistance). This produces an increase in the speed of the combined currents on the underside of the ball (with currents flowing in the same direction) and a reduction in speed on the top side (against the currents).

On the top of the ball there is an attendant increase in pressure with slow wind speeds and on the underside, a corresponding decrease in pressure (a Bernoulli effect). This pressure differential works as a force Q (Magnus force) directed downward. The degree of Magnus force depends on the ball's velocity (quadratic) and on its spin (simple).

The effect of Magnus force in the direction of gravity entails the following consequences for the ball's trajectory (see fig. 38):

- In comparison with a ball that has no spin at the same departure angle and speed, the trajectory is shorter and lower. This explains why it's possible even for balls with a high departure speed and a safe height over the net to land within bounds during play and inside the service court on a serve.
- To attain the same distance as with a hit that imparts no spin, the speed of the hit and the departure angle must be significantly greater.
- The ball generally bounces more steeply onto the court surface than does a ball with no spin.
- The angle at which the ball leaves the racket can be increased by swinging the racket more steeply upward.

Ball with Backspin

The racket is swung against the ball from behind and above in a forward and downward direction. Upon contact, the racket face must remain essentially vertical.

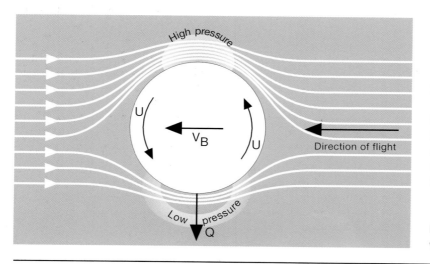

Fig. 37 Air currents and Magnus force with topspin.

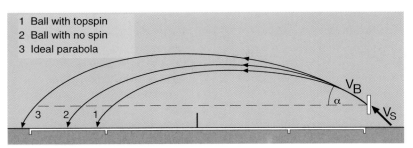

1 Ball with topspin
2 Ball with no spin
3 Ideal parabola

Fig. 38 Flight curve of a ball with topspin.

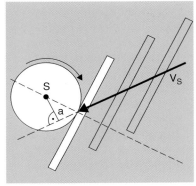

Fig. 39 Backspin with open racket face.

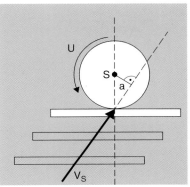

Fig. 41 Ball with left sidespin.

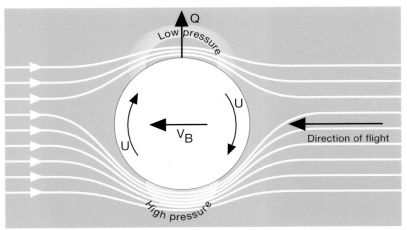

Fig. 40 Air currents and magnus force with backspin.

The direction of the hitting impulse points not at the center of the ball, but rather, below it. As a result, the ball picks up backspin. The amount of spin depends on the speed of the racket head at the moment of contact and on the greater or lesser degree of its downward movement. When the racket is swung against the ball with an open racket face (as in fig. 39), it imparts backspin to the ball. In this case, the departure angle increases.

Effect of Backspin on the Ball's Trajectory

Air currents are reversed in comparison with a topspin ball (see fig. 40). This produces a Magnus force directed upward. The following consequences are produced for the ball's trajectory:

- In comparison with the flight of a ball with no spin or with topspin, the trajectory at the same departure angle and velocity is longer and higher. This makes it possible to attain greater distance with less expenditure of force.
- The height of the trajectory can be altered by changing the swing direction of the racket (steeper or flatter) and by changing the position of the racket face at the instant of contact.
- Usually, the departure is shallower (at a more acute angle) than with shots using no spin or with topspin shots.

Ball with Sidespin

A ball picks up sidespin when the impulse of the hit is directed left or right of its center of gravity. With left sidespin, the Magnus force is directed to the left side. With right spin, it is directed to the right. This makes the ball fly in an arc to the left or the right (with left or right spin, respectively). Pure sidespin does not usually occur in actual play. It is always combined to a greater or lesser degree with topspin and backspin.

Contact Between the Ball and the Court Surface

When the tennis ball contacts the surface of the opposing court, its spin, velocity, and angle of bounce change with respect to its original angle of departure. The following paragraphs will examine these changes for a ball that has no spin and for balls with topspin, backspin, and sidespin.

Ball with No Spin

When a ball bounces onto the court, friction from skidding on the surface works to change its flight direction and give it topspin after the bounce. For the moment, this discussion will postpone explaining the effect of different court surfaces and the relationship between hardness and speed. For now we can conclude that:

- the ball picks up topspin in a bounce (see fig. 42);
- the angle of flight before a bounce is not crucial in determining the subsequent angle of bounce; and
- in a bounce the takeoff speed is slightly lower than the landing speed.

Ball with Topspin

While a ball with very little topspin behaves much like a ball with no spin, the situation differs greatly for a ball that has heavy topspin. The effect of the spin rate is connected to the effect of friction on the surface of the court. The ball spins faster as it skids on the surface and bounces off (see fig. 43). As a result:

- topspin increases when the ball bounces;
- the takeoff angle is smaller than the landing angle (see fig. 44); and
- as the vertical portion of the velocity decreases, its horizontal portion increases; therefore, the ball bounces quickly toward the opposing player.

Fig. 42   Creation of spin as a ball without spin bounces.

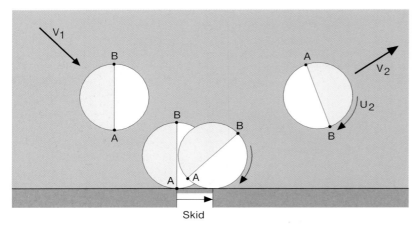

Fig. 43   Change in a ball's spin with heavy topspin.

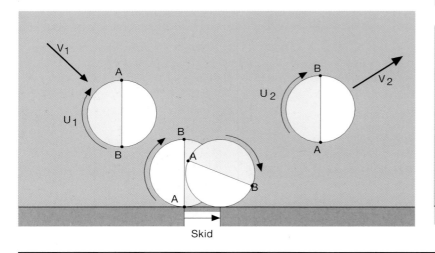

Fig. 44   Change in takeoff angle of a ball with heavy topspin.

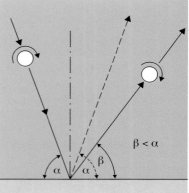

Ball with Backspin

The effect of the ball's spin rate is directed against the friction of the court surface. As the ball skids on the surface, it picks up spin and its spin direction reverses (see fig. 45). As a result:

- backspin is usually transformed into topspin when the ball bounces off the surface of the court;
- with respect to the court surface, the ball's takeoff angle is greater than its landing angle (fig. 46);
- takeoff speed is lower than landing speed; and
- the skidding effect is more pronounced than with a topspin ball.

The fact that the takeoff angle increases with backspin balls and decreases with topspin balls seems to contradict subjective observation. However, the conclusion that a ball with backspin bounces lower, even though its takeoff angle logically increases, is not really contradictory. Since a backspin ball necessarily lands at a shallower angle than a topspin ball, the bounce is perceived as shallow even though the angle increases (see fig. 47).

Ball with Sidespin

The sidespin portion of the spin combination imparted by hitting the ball causes a bounce to the left in the case of left sidespin and to the right with right sidespin.

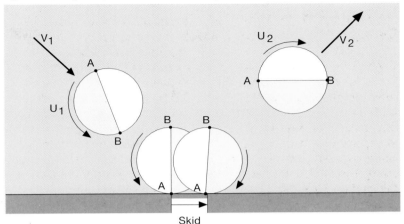

Fig. 45 Change of spin in takeoff of a backspin ball.

Skid

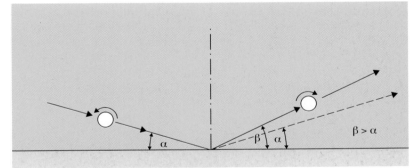

Fig. 46 Change in takeoff angle of a backspin ball.

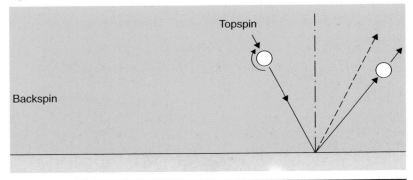

Fig. 47 Differing height of bounce with topspin and backspin balls.

Topspin

Backspin

Observations Concerning the Characteristics of Oncoming Balls

This text previously examined the effect of a hit on the ball's trajectory, independent of its speed, direction, and spin prior to contact with the racket. Naturally, these factors affect the ball and its ultimate trajectory.

Velocity and Direction of Oncoming Balls

It has already been established that the velocity of a ball in flight depends on racket speed, the ball's elasticity, the stringing and construction of the racket, and the velocity of the oncoming ball.

The flight velocity of a ball that has been hit is increased by the greater distortion of the ball and its cover when it travels at a higher speed. The sum of the speeds of the racket and the oncoming ball rarely exceeds about 100 miles (160 km) an hour. That produces a pressure of a little more than 66 pounds (30 kg) on the racket, and the hand must deal with this force. For example, a racket that hits an oncoming ball traveling 55 miles per hour (80 km/h) will not itself exceed about 50 miles (80 km) an hour.

With an oncoming ball that has little spin, as the ball gains speed, the law of reflection stating that the angle of entry equals the angle of departure becomes more evident when the racket speed is relatively low (see fig. 48). That applies for all the following:

- volleys on very fast oncoming balls (see photo, p. 51);
- half volleys on very fast oncoming balls;
- returns after very fast serves; and
- defense against smashes hit just after a bounce.

The departure angle thus nearly corresponds to the oncoming angle of the ball when the racket blocks the trajectory of the ball. If the racket is swung slowly against the ball, the departure angle is somewhat greater than the oncoming angle (see fig. 48).

As racket speed increases, the departure direction of the ball increasingly coincides with the direction of racket swing and is perpendicular to the racket face (see fig. 49). This is even more applicable at a lower ball velocity before contact. The practical application for this is with:

- service;
- smash; and
- slow oncoming baseline ground strokes.

From the foregoing, one can conclude that the direction of an oncoming ball has an effect on its subsequent direction only if the oncoming ball is traveling very fast and the racket speed is relatively low.

Spin of Oncoming Balls

As the section about bounce characteristics pointed out, every ball possesses forward spin after it bounces onto the court surface and always meets the racket with this type of spin. The only balls that have backspin at contact are ones that have been hit with backspin and that are played directly as volleys or smashes, with no intervening bounce.

Given the same racket position, a ball that has topspin when it's hit flies higher than a ball with backspin. The influence of spin is greater when:

- the spin is particularly heavy at the moment of contact (for example, when using extreme topspin shots); or
- the racket speed is relatively low (as with volleys).

Spin increases when a player responds with particularly high racket speed, as with smashes and very fast baseline shots. Sidespin changes the flight direction to the side but only when the sidespin is especially heavy. This applies only in the case of defense against service with sidespin:

- a ball with left sidespin (for example, slice service from a right-handed player) changes its flight direction slightly toward the left);
- a ball with right spin (for example, slice service from a left-handed player) flies to the right; especially after bouncing on fast court surfaces, these balls retain their sidespin.

The position of the racket face determines the departure direction of a fast oncoming ball with no spin.

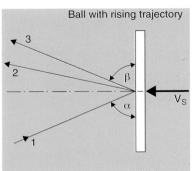

Ball with rising trajectory

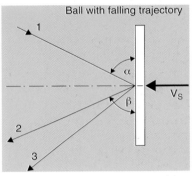

Ball with falling trajectory

Fig. 48 Direction of departure with high ball velocity and low racket speed (1: direction of approach; 2: departure direction; 3: departure direction with blocked racket).

Fig. 49 Departure direction at high racket speed and low ball velocity (1: direction of approach; 2: departure direction; 3: departure direction with blocked racket).

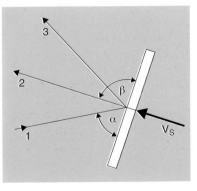

Tactics

Tactics play an important role in tennis just as they do in all types of ball sports. **Tactics involve purposeful application of techniques to any given situation. This presupposes that thought processes are used to arrive at various appropriate decisions based on perception and evaluation.**

Every individual structuring of the game, which must take into account such factors as temperament, motivation, cleverness, technical requirements, physical conditioning, outlook on the game, the opponent, and environmental conditions including weather, court surface, and the significance of the tournament, must also involve tennis-specific considerations:

- safety and accuracy should take precedence over speed;
- only in rare cases can the ball be hit at top speed, such as with a smash or a high volley; all other shots, including service, can be played at only an optimal speed based on the size of the court and the height of the net;
- the more highly developed an individual technique is, the greater the tactical variations

- creativity, risk acceptance, and competitive aggressiveness, independent of the player's individual conception of the game, are characteristics that define performance in contemporary sports;
- use of theoretically perfect tactics to achieve any outcome is not always possible or reasonable; trying to find a solution that takes into account all specific requirements and that is achievable is important.

Tactics and Strategy

These two terms are often interchanged, so pointing out the difference between them is important. In sports literature, the term *tactics* is generally used as a main heading, while *strategy* is a subcategory of that heading.

Tactical Actions

Tactical actions are based on the following processes:

- perception and anticipation;

- evaluating the resulting possible actions;
- choosing one of these possible actions.

Perception can be divided into two areas:
Perception after one's own shot:
- position during the shot;
- direction, speed, and placement of the ball;
- the opponent's starting position, direction of run, and preparation for the shot.

Perception after the opponent's shot:
- direction, velocity, spin, and placement of the oncoming ball;
- distance from the contact point and direction of run;
- movement and new position of opponent (probably by peripheral vision).

With anticipation, which involves guessing or reading in advance the opponent's intentions, the following *preconditions* apply:
- knowledge of the opponent's usual behaviors in typical situations;
- knowledge of the opponent's habits and individual behavioral patterns.

Tactics

The following observations are necessary for utilizing this knowledge to produce the desired results:

Orientation characteristics:
- the player's position on the court;
- preparation for the shot (movement toward the contact point, grip, foot placement, and backswing);
- positioning at the moment the ball is hit (in front of or behind the baseline, and so on);
- type of hit (direction of spin and velocity);
- location of the contact point (low, high, close or far to the side, or in front of, beside, or behind the body).

Perceptions must first be evaluated based on experience and knowledge in order to choose the actions that will follow.

This process means that tactical actions are closely connected to thought processes. The thought process in tennis must be especially rapid. It also takes place under great physical and psychological demands, because the sport requires fast actions and reactions. Once this is recognized, distinguishing various types of thought from one another and assigning them such terms as *tactics* and *intelligence* become possible.

Intuitive thought involves immediately grasping information, usually under extreme time pressure, and formulating a single, closely circumscribed course of action in response to the information processed. For example, in a volley at the net, the ball may be hit in such a way that the opponent is caught on the wrong foot. The player of the volley has anticipated where the opponent, who could not reflect on the situation because of time constraints, was going to run. The opponent thus had no opportunity to think through the possible actions. More often tennis involves frequently rehearsed thoughts and actions that have become automatic. Most individual actions performed under time pressure can be classified as this type of thought.

Whenever adequate time is available to plan actions and weigh them against one another, allowing the player to arrive at one decision among several possibilities, *operative thought* is occurring. Actions are carried out internally in one's thoughts to evaluate their effectiveness in the given situation.

Before the serve, a player can consider if a fast but risky shot is called for or if heavy topspin will succeed in catching the opponent off guard. Operative thinking refers to individual actions in the absence of tremendous time pressure. However, operative thinking can also occur within the framework of a series of actions when time is crucial. That means that in a fairly long rally, a player has to consider what actions or operations the rally should end with in order to be successful.

When such a chain of actions is embedded in a complex unfolding of events free of undue time pressure and when the player formulates plans of action (that is, *strategies*) for an entire match or if the overall strategy changes because it is not working, then the player is using *strategic thinking*.

Intuitive, operative, and strategic thinking constitute *tactics.* Tactical abilities are performance-limiting factors. They need to be adjusted to the player's competitive goals and especially to the behavior of the player's opponent. These tactical abilities can thus be exemplified by different levels of action, according to whether intuitive, operative, or strategic thinking is required.

Intuitive, operative, and strategic thinking also comprise *sport-specific intelligence.* Abilities specific to tennis players are known as game intelligence. The simplest form of game intelligence consists of employing intuitive thinking to select individual actions that will further the player's competitive goals. For example, a player may try to catch the opponent off balance, stop a volley, or use a topspin lob to outplay an opponent standing at the net. The more operative and strategic thinking are called for, the greater the demand to deal with new situations, resolve problems through analysis and insight, and turn the situation around so that a solution is found in the nature of the problem.

Thinking through the various possible actions leads to choosing the most promising solution.

This section must reiterate that thinking tactically, or coming up with successful tactical actions, highly depends on the quality of one's technique. In regard to strategic planning, the player's strengths should be a primary consideration. If these strengths do not produce the desired result, the opponent's strengths, weaknesses, and ways of thinking should be considered. Players who, over time, want to be victorious in a majority of matches need to develop their technical strengths and the attendant ways of thinking into effective tools.

Basic Tactical Situations

In principle, five basic tactical situations occur:
- simple exchanges of shots:
  This usually involves a rally from baseline to baseline with no particular advantages or disadvantages for either player.
- applying pressure:
  The player stands at or in front of the baseline and plays:
  – high and long to the opponent's baseline (and with heavy topspin);
  – hard into the corners of the opponent's court;
  – short and at sharp angles.
- attack:
  The player is in a good position, usually in front of the baseline,

and tries to use an attack stroke to get into a promising position at the net or to score a point directly.
- counterattack:
  A well-controlled offensive shot can be used as a counterattack if the opponent's attack shot is weak or if the player is very effective in anticipating the attack shot.
- defense:
  The player is no longer able to get into a good position and make a controlled shot.

This is usually the sequence in which a point is scored.

Central, Overriding Tactical Goals

Overriding tactical goals involve the criteria of space and time:
- space:
  The goal is to restrict the opponent's space by playing positions effectively (for example, on the bisector of the angle of the best possible return shots) and denying the opponent opportunities to place the ball effectively and score points. The player must also attempt, by means of well-placed shots, to force the opponent to run far—even out of bounds—thereby widening the playing space and freeing up more area for play.
- time:
  The goal is to afford as little time as possible for the opponent to act. This is accomplished by

hitting the ball early or at high speed. The player must also try to have as much time as possible to make choices and execute appropriate actions.

Individual and General Tactical Behaviors

Based on different conditions such as mentality, temperament, motor skills, and conditioning, each player develops *an individual repertory of tactical behaviors.* One player may tend to hit a passing ball down the line in certain situations; another may hit a cross passing shot in a similar situation. This especially happens when time is short and the player must act *intuitively.*

At the same time, independently of individualized solutions players may choose in particular situations, there are some *general tactical behaviors* that make classifying players into four groups possible:

1. Serve and Volley Players
These are distinguished by the following characteristics:
- very strong first serve, with which points can be scored directly or that can provoke mistakes in returns;
- the first and second serves place the returning player under permanent pressure so that the server can play the majority of first volleys to good advantage;

– a high percentage of successful first volleys;
– very good perception and anticipation materially increase the chances of intercepting the opponent's passing shots at the net; that places the opponent under pressure and significantly increases that player's likelihood of making mistakes;
– a strong smash from all positions;
– very good leg power combined with a highly developed sense of balance.

In the realm of world-class tennis, this group of players (currently represented especially by Edberg), who play serve and volley on all types of surfaces, is continually shrinking.

2. All-Court Players

These are distinguished by the following characteristics:
– an ability to play serve and volley or from the baseline, depending on court surface;
– great safety and precision in baseline shots and returns;
– an ability to play continually up close to the net and to contact the ball regularly at or before its highest point;
– an ability to attack shorter shots by the opponent and score points (winners) directly or to play attack shots;
– very good coordination and exceptional conditioning.

In contemporary tennis, this group of players is quite heavily populated and is among the most successful in international competition. Names such as Becker, Ivanisevic, Krajicek, Sampras,

Stick, Novotna, Sabatini, Sukova, and many others belong to this group. Interestingly, nearly all players in this category play backhand with one hand.

3. Baseline Players

These are distinguished by the following characteristics:
– reliable and aggressive baseline strokes in forehand and backhand;
– an ability to control the game from the baseline and to keep the opponent under pressure;
– an ability to play at the baseline and in front of it and to contact the ball as often as possible at or before its highest point (including half volley);
– great accuracy even with balls traveling at high speed;
– playing the angles very effectively;
– an ability to hit aggressive but safe returns;
– an ability to hit passing balls well;
– great speed and a finely developed sense of balance.

This group of players is growing larger, and, in particular, the youngest generation of players tend to this type of play. Players such as Graf, Hingis, Huber, Pierce, Sanchez-Vicario, Agassi, Chang, Courier, Kafelnikov, and Medvedev support that observation. In contrast with the group of all-court players, most of these athletes, except for Graf, play the backhand with two hands.

4. Defensive Players

These players are distinguished by the following characteristics:

– heavy topspin shots from the baseline in forehand and backhand;
– playing positions fairly far behind the baseline;
– reliable and exceptionally consistent play using baseline shots;
– use of few offensive and attack shots;
– good running ability and endurance;
– lots of patience and self-discipline.

Players in this category are seldom encountered at the pinnacle of international competition, but formerly it included Borg and Vilas. Of course, some players change from one category to another over time, or are borderline cases, such as Bruguera. Court surfaces of different speeds also force players to modify their tactics accordingly.

In the future, world-class tennis will clearly be dominated by all-court and baseline players.

Tactical Quality

Independent of which category a player belongs to, establishing a criterion that can be used for evaluating all types of strategic and tactical behaviors is imperative. This criterion involves *tactical quality,* which consists of two components:
• the right choice of spatial goal in the opponent's court in any given situation (long shot to the baseline, short cross, and so on) with the accompanying ball flight (that is, fast, slow, high, or low).

- choice of the right type of stroke with reference to the selected spatial goal and the desired trajectory of the ball (for example, topspin, slice, drop shot, or lob).

In evaluating the tactical quality of a shot or an entire action, the *technical* considerations of shoulder position, arm bend, footwork, and so forth, are not brought into play. The important thing is the mental choice of direction, speed, type of shot, and other such factors in the applicable situation.

Offensive and Defensive Shots

With *offensive shots,* the players have very good control. The shots are made consciously, they have a purpose, and they are played at maximum speed. These shots can be made from any position on the court by using all possible stroke techniques and variations. The players have the necessary time to analyze the situation and make decisions. They are not forced into a limited range of actions by the situation or the opponent. The players can act of their own volition. The success of their action depends solely on the quality of their tactical decision and its technical execution.

Defensive shots are not subject to optimal control. An awkward stroke position, a difficult shot, or the opponent's position greatly reduces the player's options. Oftentimes, only one action is possible from a technical or tactical standpoint. The players are subordinate to the situation and can only *react.*

The tactical goal should therefore involve bringing the opponent as often as possible into situations where defensive shots are the only recourse; this allows the player to make as many offensive shots as possible. The decisive factor in achieving this goal is the technical quality of the shots in combination with optimal speed and great accuracy.

The Significance of Individual Points and Plays

Extensive statistical evidence demonstrates that the concepts about important points (big points) and the deciding scores (the seventh game) scarcely have any basis in fact. The player who scores the greatest number of points in the crucial scores does not automatically become the eventual winner. Players who believe in favorable or unfavorable scores place themselves under unnecessary pressure. They consider an unfavorable score as a threat and react with caution, anxiety, passiveness, nervousness, or lack of confidence and concentration. With favorable scores, they play with pluck, resolve, energy, aggressiveness, heightened concentration, and reasonable risk acceptance. Most matches are won by the player who:
- scores the absolute majority of all points played;
- can accumulate the greatest number of series of three and more points in succession.

Every point is therefore important, regardless of score. Players should not give points away lightly but, rather, try their hardest with *every rally* to score each point as if it were the last.

Relationship Between Tactics and Technique

Players should put into practice only those techniques that they can master technically. This means that tactical actions and strategic planning must always function within the framework of available technical skills. With time and technical development, tactics can also be perfected a step at a time.

Safety

The first prerequisite for scoring points in a game is safety. At any level of play, the competitor who makes the fewer forced errors generally wins. This means that with every decision, with every tactical action, the reliability factor must be paramount. This involves safety with reference to ball speed, placement, and the player's risk assumption.

Calculated Risk

Insistence on safety does not need to be so extreme that it excludes all risk. On the contrary, without some calculated risk a player can scarcely surprise the opponent or apply any pressure. Calculated risk signifies imaginativeness within the framework of a player's technical potential and the momentary situation on the court.

Patience

Ill-considered, hasty, or rash decisions lead to mishaps. Every tactical action should thus be programmed so that shots and progressions of play are well thought out and successful. Winning a point should not be left to chance. Rather, it must be worked for systematically and in accordance with the situation, the player's position, and the momentary circumstances. Players therefore need to exercise patience.

Concentration

Concentration is a decisive factor not only for the best possible technical execution but also for successful tactical moves. In a rally, players have to concentrate on the ball and avoid getting distracted.

Variability

Variability signifies flexibility in previously established strategic planning rather than variability among different tactical behaviors. A plan that works well at the start of a match can lose its effectiveness if used with stubborn determination and no variety. Without moments of surprise, a player will eventually become transparent; the opponent will therefore pick up on the player's game plan. This means that certain variations should be foreseen from the beginning in strategic planning. Additionally, players should be in a position to change their entire strategic concept if it ceases to be effective.

Discipline

Self-discipline is certainly the most important of the basic prerequisites for consistent play. This especially applies to inner tension (nervousness) and to external pressure applied by an opponent. Self-discipline involves both the performance of an individual shot as well as the exact contents of a strategic plan.

Fundamental Tactical Elements

These involve conditions that facilitate tactical actions.

Starting Stance/ Ready Position

A correct ready position is a prerequisite for a proper and speedy start in any direction. Different ready positions correspond to various typical play situations, and these must be assumed as required. Essentially, this involves the serve, return, baseline play, and net play.

Service Position

In serving, players stand between 1 foot and 1.5 feet (0.3 to 0.5 m) to the left or right of the center mark of the baseline, depending on the point to which they usually serve.

They approach the midpoint more if they want to target point *1* (in fig. 50). If the serve is to be placed farther out (as at point *2*), the ready position is accordingly shifted toward the outside.

The player must continue to use the chosen position for all

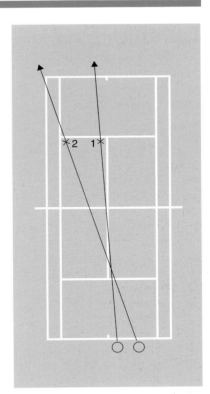

Fig. 50

directions so that the opponent cannot tell beforehand where a shot will go.

Position on a Return

Normally, a player should wait for the serve about 1 yard (1 m) behind the baseline and at the middle of the angle (see position *P*, fig. 51) of the best possible serves. This position can be shifted left or right, or backward or forward, in accordance with the opponent's technical ability and reactions. The speed and angle of the oncoming shot can also be shifted to allow for the most effective return.

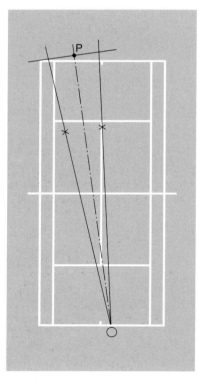

Fig. 51

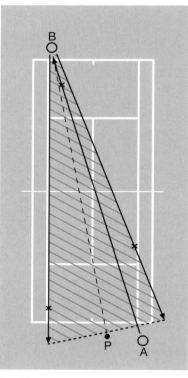

Fig. 52

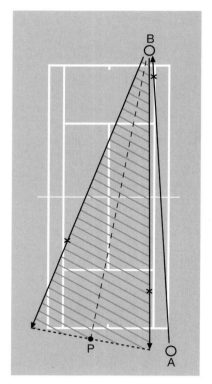

Fig. 53

The returning player must move ahead when the server tosses the ball up and take a split step when the server hits the ball. This allows the player to react effectively in any direction.

Position for Baseline Play

A player who is in continual motion usually remains about 1 to 3 feet (0.5 to 1 m) behind the baseline. A position farther back makes reaching short shots and hitting them on the rise or at their highest point harder to accomplish.

As figure 52 shows, a player waits for the opponent's backhand shot after a cross shot from the forehand corner about 1.5 feet (0.5 m) to the right of the baseline center mark. After a shot down

the line, the ideal position for covering the court would be a little more than 1 foot (0.5 m) to the left of that (fig. 53). The middle of the angle of the best possible returns by player B passes through point P. That produces the shorter or longer route to the corresponding position P, the best spot for covering one's own court. Fortunately, as has been determined empirically, after a shot down the line, waiting for the return at the midpoint of the baseline is sufficient.

Position for Net Play

Except when playing doubles, taking up a position at the net is not easy. A player has to fight to gain that position. This can be done by following the trajectory of the attack shot or the serve to

the net. There the player attempts to assume the position that will pose the greatest chance of covering the court from the opponent's passing shots or lobs (see fig. 54 and 55). That would involve all positions along the $B–P_1$ angle bisector in the case of a cross-court attacking shot or along $B–P_2$ for an attack down the line.

For a volley, a player should move up to the net as close as possible since the court is easier to cover from up close. The distance from the net will vary greatly among individuals. It is determined by the player's reaction time, size, and leg strength since even lobs need to be covered.

The participant must be in the ready position (or turntable position) before the opponent hits the

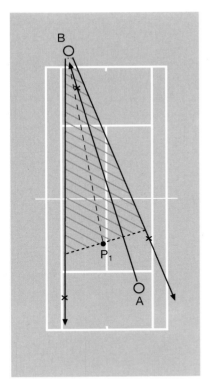

Fig. 54

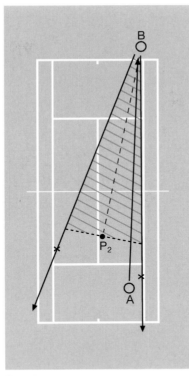

Fig. 55

possible. Therefore, the player should avoid using the weak side—the backhand, in this instance—whenever possible.

Attacking Weaknesses

A player should focus on playing the opponent's weaknesses. This applies to baseline play, service, and even the passing shot (which is aimed at the weaker volley side) and the volley, which should be played on the weaker passing shot side.

Naturally, the weakness should be targeted only if the situation makes it possible and the individual technical requirements are in place to deliver the shot perfectly. If in doubt or under pressure, always use the most reliable shot!

Adaptable Play

Every opportunity that presents itself should be seized. In certain circumstances, that means that the player has to change tactics on short notice. A baseline player must go up to the net for a short, weak shot by the opponent to connect with a volley. However, using caution is advised. A short ball played with regularity may be a ruse to lure a player to the net so that the opponent can use a strength shot such as a passing shot.

Variation

If the opponent adapts to the types of play outlined above, a player can vary the direction, tempo, height, and even the type of shot. However, the player should in no case change simply for the sake of variety. Rather, variation should be used to upset the timing and rhythm of the opponent.

passing ball. Therefore, especially with an attack from service, waiting for the ball a little farther to the rear, rather than rushing forward too hastily, is recommended.

A Safe Shot

When players find themselves under pressure or in a tight situation, they should play any shot they have mastered.
• for baseline and net play, safety involves:
cross-court shots; controllable stroke tempo; a distance of 3 feet (1 m) from the line and over the net; use of the most familiar type of shot, in other words, avoidance of risky shot combinations;
• for service:
keep the first serve in the court by paying attention

to placement and distance; a controlled stroke improves reliability of the shot.

The self-discipline mentioned above is important in these instances. Accepting that in some situations a player can experience success only by neutralizing a rally (such as by returning the ball high) is not easy. Answering pressure with counterpressure is very exciting, but it is often too risky and tactically wrong.

Using One's Own Strengths

Most players have developed a particular shot that is much more effective than the others, and that may be a real winning shot. This strength, such as a forehand drive, should be used as frequently as

Percentage Tennis

In any situation, a player should always use the shot that promises the best results. That means that a passing shot should be chosen before a lob if the passing shot has an 80 percent chance of success as compared 50 percent for the lob.

Sticking with Successful Tactics

If a player experiences success with a particular stroke technique such as topspin or a system of play (such as stopping the ball), then continuing to play that way is usually a good idea. In view of an imminent victory, resisting an attempt to introduce variations is often difficult. In other words, never change a winning game. This also applies when the successful tactic consists of continual variation. In that case, keep changing things.

External Influences on Tactics

Sun

In using the lob or in choosing sides, a player should take into consideration the position of the sun. One player may be required to serve into the sun. Having the sun at the player's back is better for a lob or an attack. Caution is advised in attempting a smash against the sun. If in doubt, letting the ball bounce is better.

Wind

A player who is not a net stormer should play primarily from the baseline when the wind is strong. Balls should not be too low or too long, especially with a tailwind, but rather should be played to the middle of the court. A head wind will require hitting the ball harder.

If hitting a passing ball in a crosswind becomes necessary, a cross shot should be the choice. Use a shot down the line only with the wind and a lob only into the wind.

It is difficult to volley and smash well in the wind. The ball may travel faster or slower (in other words, shorter). With a crosswind, players must sometimes be prepared to hit a passing shot at the outer limit of their reach and at other times closer to their body than expected.

Surface Composition

Without question, a slow, soft surface serves to heighten the effect of a slice (causing the ball to bounce flatter) or a drop shot (where the ball bounces lower). In addition, the dreaded winner shot will be only partly effective. Baseline strategies have some advantages in this instance. Playing serve and volley is riskier since the opponent has more time for a well-placed passing ball. On the other hand, on a fast, hard surface, where the ball bounces higher, topspin and the slice attack (where the ball bounces lower) begin to resemble service shots and point winners. Here the advantage goes to active players with good reactions.

Using Tactics

Basic tactics are applied to certain shots or progressions of play according to the opportunities that arise in order to maximize effective play in any type of rally. The next section will look at some recurring situations.

Service

Using the Serve

The type, tempo, direction, and distance of the serve determine its quality. The majority of serves should be directed at the side where the weaker return is expected. Players should serve using any technique they have fully mastered, especially when the pressure is on (for example, because of score). Thus, a long, well-placed, rather slow first serve is always preferable to a riskier one. This is even more applicable to the second serve, which moreover should be played with significant spin.

Effect of Shot Direction

The direction of the serve can influence the direction of the anticipated return. Figure 56 shows the following. The line covered by server A after the serve scarcely changes at all; this is independent of whether the serve is directed to point 1 or 2. The size of the area encompassed by lines a and b, or a_1 and b_1 or a_2 and b_2 is just about the same. The relationship between a_1 and a_2 or b_1 and b_2 has, however, changed significantly.

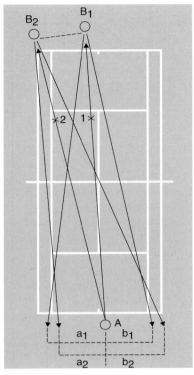

Fig. 56

With a serve to point *1*, the server has less area to cover with a forehand shot and a little more with a backhand. However, with a serve to point *2*, the area to cover with a forehand shot is larger (b_2), and the area to cover with a backhand is smaller (a_2). A backhand hitter can also be forced to deal with the server's stronger side in certain situations.

In addition to a serve directed at the forehand or backhand side, the possibility arises of serving directly at the opponent's body. Some players, especially if they are not particularly agile, have trouble with balls aimed right at their body. That is why this shot should always be part of a good player's arsenal.

Straight (First) Serve

A straight serve (without sidespin) is effective only as a fast serve. It should therefore be used only as a first serve.

The straight serve is as effective on the outside as the inside. In the former case, it forces the opponent out of the court. Many players try to hit an ace with an inside ball since the net is lower in the middle and the trajectory is shorter.

Serves directed to the outside corners could be played a little shorter or more to the outside. However, a serve to the inside, particularly one aimed at the opponent, should be played as long as possible, that is, close to the service line. That makes a return to the left or right the more difficult.

Slice Service

On dirt courts, the slice service is usually used only as a second serve. On the other hand, on fast courts (hard court, carpeting, and so on), which accentuate flat bouncing characteristics, it is also regularly used as a first serve.

This applies especially to service from the right on the forehand side, which opens the opposing court more than the straight serve. As a variation, the slice service can be played from the right to the inside since from the viewpoint of a right-hander, the shot curves toward the opponent's body. This can create problems as the opponent tries to control the return.

Topspin Service

Topspin service (kick service) is of inestimable worth as a safe second serve since it clears the net higher than the slice service and the straight serve. It is particularly effective on hard courts, which accentuate the ball's bounce. It forces the opponent to play high backhand shots, which are technically difficult, or to assume a defensive position far behind the baseline.

Return

Use of the Return

The return has become the most important shot in tennis. In top-level tennis, a break usually leads to winning a set. Since a return is always a reaction to the opponent's service, recognizing the opponent's intention as quickly as possible in order to respond to it is essential.

To assume a good ready position for a return—a prerequisite for an effective return—a player has to watch the opponent closely just before the serve. This includes the toss of the ball as well as the opponent's position. If the opponent shoots from the right and close to the center mark, then the player should move closer to the middle to cover more effectively a ball that comes to the backhand. In certain circumstances, the opponent may be forced to serve to a particular corner (especially with the second serve). This assumes that the player wants to provoke a serve from the right to the strong forehand side. In that case, the player leaves the service court on the right up to two-thirds uncovered by assuming a position farther to the left beside the normal ready position. Even if the opponent further tries to serve to the closely confined backhand side, which causes problems even for good players, a majority of serves will nevertheless land on the strong forehand side.

With this maneuver, the player still has to be wary of the serve consciously directed to the outside, to the strong side. An experienced adversary will serve to that point in order to force the player back to the middle, to the normal ready position.

Defensive Return

On a very good serve, it is often a positive outcome if the opponent wins no direct service point. The return of a good serve should therefore be safe: not too flat (which is risky) and preferably played across the court to keep the opponent from coming up to the net.

An appropriate alternative would be a lob if the opponent remains at the baseline after serving.

The harder the opponent's serve and the less time available for a backswing on the return, the more using a short take back and blocking the shot is recommended.

Common Return

Several possibilities are available in placing a return. If the server pauses at the baseline, a long return to the baseline is recommended. That forces the opponent to make the subsequent shot from behind the baseline. It excludes the immediate danger of a particularly

aggressive attack shot. If the server comes up to the net, a return down the line is effective. This forces the server to stretch to the limit and causes making the shot to be much harder. However, these returns are also risky. If they are not performed properly, they leave the field open for a cross volley.

A return to the attacker's feet should always be part of a player's repertory, especially since from the viewpoint of a net player, it constitutes an especially awkward return. The lob is also an alternative that can be used in this instance.

Offensive Return

A weak second serve on the part of the opponent should be treated like a baseline shot that falls short: as an opportunity to attack or a chance to put on some pressure. On this type of return, the player moves up a step or two—perhaps circumventing a backhand—hits the ball hard into the corner, and, depending on the situation, either stays back or follows the shot to the net.

Variations can involve a drop return, which may also be very effective. Right after a weak second serve, the opponent will find getting to a good drop shot very difficult.

Baseline Play

Baseline play dominates on dirt courts. This explains why baseline play takes on special significance that affects its tactical application.

A Safe Baseline Shot

A whole array of situations occur where playing the ball back safely is tactically correct. These include:

- when the opponent places the ball far into the corners;
- when the opponent plays the ball long and at the baseline;
- when the opponent's tempo puts pressure onto the player;
- when an impatient opponent can be induced into making risky shots;
- when the opponent is not very tenacious or confident with the ball.

The goal of safe baseline shots therefore involves:

- keeping the opponent back;
- avoiding mistakes;
- causing the opponent to make mistakes;
- tiring opponents who are not physically fit;
- putting pressure onto the opponent.

Shot Direction

The safe direction is across the court, because:

- the net is lower in the middle;
- the diagonal of a tennis court is longer than the sideline, so longer shots are possible (by about 4 feet (1.25 m);
- the safe play area is about equal on both sides (with shots down the line, only up to midcourt);
- covering a return against a cross shot is easier (see fig. 52 and 53).

As can be seen in the illustrations on page 60, the distance from A, where the ball is hit, to the optimal position P for covering the court after a cross shot is significantly shorter than the distance to the corresponding position for a ball hit down the line. The savings in time is especially important when a player is under pressure from the opponent.

Length of Shot, Height of Trajectory, and Shot Speed

The ball must be *long* in order to keep the opponent at the baseline. It is *long* when it bounces in the vicinity of the baseline so that an opponent who is not taking any chances cannot play it back as an attack shot (for example, from the net). Length is achieved by trying to play back at the same height and at the same or a greater shot speed the balls that always fall too short, bouncing at midcourt. Since this section is discussing safe baseline shots, the length of the shot should be carefully controlled for height. The appropriate combination of height and length (depending on the type of shot) is best determined in training. A safe, long ball should be played about 3 to 6 feet (1 to 2 m) over the net and no closer than 3 feet (1 m) in front of the baseline to avoid landing out-of-bounds. At the same time, it should bounce at least 3 feet (1 m) behind midcourt. Figure 57 shows why that is particularly important. Not only does the shot angle increase as the player approaches the net, the distance that the player must run left or right on the baseline also increases. Instead of the

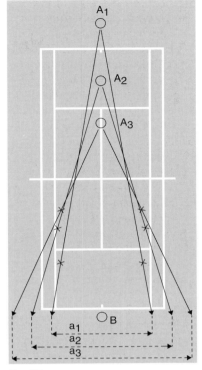

Fig. 57

three or four running steps left or right when the ball is played from A_1, the player must take five or more steps when the ball comes from A_2 or A_3.

Type of Shot

Although in theory every type of shot is equally reliable, players should choose the shot they have mastered most completely for a safe baseline shot.

"Offensive" Baseline Shot

Many situations arise in which playing the ball back offensively (that is, fast) and accepting a certain amount of risk is tactically advantageous. Examples include:

- when the opponent is playing too short;
- when the opponent has a significant weakness in backhand or forehand;
- when the player has an opportunity to run around the weaker backhand;
- when the opponent is slow.

The goal of a fast baseline shot should therefore be:

- to force to opponent out of position;
- to cause the opponent to make mistakes by playing fast;
- to attack the opponent on the weaker side;
- to score direct points.

Shot Speed

Foremost among shot characteristics is speed. The player attempts to hit the ball fast and use the speed to put pressure onto the opponent. A certain amount of risk must be accepted. With this type of shot, watching how well it is working is very important. This type of approach makes sense only if the relationship between shot speed (involving risk) and success (scoring points) works out favorably. If not, shot speed should be reduced, for uncontrolled or excessively fast shots are poor shots.

Shot Length

Shot height and speed are closely connected to distance. Naturally, the long, fast ball is always desirable. However, a short cross shot to the outside can also be very effective.

Shot Direction

A specific shot direction cannot be recommended. A player shoots for the unprotected corner, to the weak spot, or against the opponent's direction of run (toward the wrong foot). That can be done with a cross or a ball down the line.

Direction-changing shots, or shots where the ball is hit in a different direction than the one from which it came, can be very successful. However, they must be done very carefully and be developed through training since they are very difficult.

Type of Shot

Even though in theory every type of shot can be made offensively (that is, fast), the type of shot that should be chosen for an offensive baseline shot is the one that the player has mastered most completely. Here must be mentioned the forehand shot from the backhand corner, even if the backhand and forehand are essentially as good as one another according to the tactical observations in this section. A fast player with good footwork who prefers to play on the forehand should take every opportunity to use this shot, which is very well suited to offensive play. This allows the player to exert great pressure on the opponent's backhand side as well as to fire shots down the line to the more vulnerable forehand side.

Passing Shot

Even when the opponent's attack shot is long and well placed, a player has a real chance to win the point with a passing shot. For that purpose, the ball should be played as flat as possible or sink after

passing over the net. Here are some applicable rules of thumb:

- the farther from the net the opponent waits for the passing shot (for example, level with the service line), the more appropriate is a cross shot;
- the closer to the net the opponent stands, the more effective a passing shot down the line is likely to be;
- however, if the opponent shows any weaknesses in a forehand or backhand volley, the passing shot should always be aimed at the weak volley side.

The best balls for passing shots are the ones that use topspin and sink after crossing the net.

Since points are earned through means other than passing shots, such as through an opponent's mistakes, the aggressiveness and risk factor in passing shots should be held in check. In other words, when in doubt, forcing the opponent into hitting a difficult volley (as in percent tennis) is better than trying to score a winner with a passing shot.

Lob

The lob should be part of every player's repertory of shots. A successful lob must be played high; the faster it falls, the harder it is to smash. It should be played long. It going out by an inch is better than having it continually fall short. Players must remember to use this type of shot.

Usually a lob is played across the court. As with a baseline shot (see p. 64), it is safer when played cross than down the line.

In addition to tactical considerations, safety of individual shots

is, of course, a decisive factor in choosing the type of shot (such as topspin or slice). The slice lob is the safest and most precise shot. A masterful topspin lob is, without doubt, the most effective shot. External factors such as sun and wind should be considered in choosing a lob (see p. 62).

Drop Shot

Here are the tactical goals addressed by a drop ball:

- scoring a point directly;
- interrupting the opponent's rhythm;
- luring the opponent to the net (weak volley);
- tiring and unnerving an out-of-shape opponent through continuous repetition of the shot.

To that end, the drop shot must:

- contain an element of surprise;
- be played short—that is, spend the shortest possible time in the air.

The stroke should be carried out in such a way that the start or take back never signals the intended shot. For that reason, the drop shot should be played only on the side (forehand or backhand) where the slice is most frequently used and is safe since at the outset a drop shot and a slice are practically identical. A drop ball should, of course, be placed as short as possible behind the net. The more vertically a drop shot falls to the other side of the net, the less it bounces to meet the opponent. This explains why the ball should not be played too flat, so it bounces up straighter.

While the opponent has a little more time to reach the shot, the drop shot also requires running forward an additional two or three steps.

The longer the ball is in flight, the better the opponent's chance of adjusting to it and reaching it. A shot hit from the baseline is riskier than one from the T-line since the opponent has more time to get to it.

Effective Tactics for Covering the Court After a Drop Shot

If the opponent reaches the drop, usually the ball will be returned long to the baseline, short across the court, or as another drop shot. After a drop shot from the baseline, the player should wait for the opponent's response about 3 feet (1 m) in front of the baseline. A counterdrop can be reached from this position. However, intercepting a long shot to the baseline is also possible.

After a drop shot from midcourt, the player should move up to the net, even closer than with an attack shot. The run to the net should follow the precise direction of the drop ball. Watch out for the lob!

Effective Tactics Against a Drop Shot

When the opponent plays a drop shot, the player does not have much time to ponder going after it. Often, a fraction of a second or a small step determines if the player can get to the ball.

As the player runs forward, the ball and the opponent should be kept in view. If the opponent is waiting for the ball behind the baseline, the player should attempt to play a counterdrop. If the opponent is a yard (meter) or two in front of the baseline, the right response would be a longer shot into a baseline corner.

Net Play

A successful player must master the tactics of net play. He or she must also possess a solid serve and a safe baseline game.

Volley

Reach, reaction time, and correct net position (distance from net and lateral displacement from boundary line) are crucial in determining the success of a volley. Since the angles for a successful volley shorten and improve with every step forward and since volleys are easier to hit from farther forward (from high to low) than from farther back (from low to high), the player must attempt to volley as close as possible to the net. The distance between the net and the contact point with the ball should not be less than about 6 feet (2 m). Otherwise, it is too easy to lob too far. In addition, the reaction time for a successful volley may be too short when the position is too close to the net. Whether the ideal net position is right on the center line or a little left or right depends on the direction of the previous attack ball. In any case, the middle of the angle of the opponent's best possible returns is crucial to the position at the net (see pp. 60–61, "Position for Net Play").

The player must jump into the ready position (split step) at the net at the instant the opponent hits the ball. This allows the player to react more effectively in any direction. It further serves to force the opponent to divert some necessary attention away from the ball and onto the player moving at the net.

The following lists some tactical rules of thumb that should be observed in playing volleys:

- A volley played near midcourt at the level of the service line should be played down the line to the baseline in preparation for a volley. Then the player should move closer to the net.
- A volley played at the level of the service line and close to the sideline should be played cross court. That gives a player more time to get into a good position for the second volley. In this special instance, covering the court most effectively is a secondary consideration, and the player moves closer to the net.
- A volley very close to the net should be hit short and across the court. This shot is not only technically easier, but above all, it is more reliable.

Many times a ball hit opposite the opponent's direction of run is very successful, especially if the opponent is slow to react or not very agile. This works only when enough time is available to react to a situation and choose a corner.

In an uncertain situation, the ball should be played into a corner from which the weaker passing shot is likely to come (see p. 61). This involves attacking the weak spot.

Smash

If a player handles volleys successfully, the opponent will try to force the attacker back with a lob to the baseline. In this case, the attacker must use a smash.

Behind the service line, players smash cross and long to the baseline; closer to the net they smash cross and short. Basically, a cross is the best choice—that is, in the direction that offers the greatest target area—since smashes down the line are often risky overhead shots. On the one hand, they are easier for the opponent to return. In addition, they frequently land out of bounds.

Even a good overhead player has to deal with smashes by the opponent. That explains why moving up and immediately after the smash getting back into the best possible net position is best.

The *backhand smash* should usually be avoided, especially if the player has not mastered it thoroughly. Almost always, a backhand smash that becomes necessary for reasons of convenience or hesitation can be hit as a forehand smash if the player simply decides to do so immediately.

Service—Net Play

Once the player starts for the net, he or she should not hesitate. In no case should a player wait to see if the serve lands in the service court before running forward. Every inch closer to the net improves the position for playing volleys.

In attacking the net, the player follows the approximate trajectory of the serve. That way the player can use the reach to best advantage and cover the court effectively. The player then assumes the ready position in order to be prepared for a volley or a smash. The tempo of the run forward must be tailored to the individual so that the participant can get into the turntable position without haste *before* the opponent plays the return.

A stable, clean, fairly aggressive volley played farther back is always preferable to a hasty volley played farther forward. After the first volley, the player should move up and resume the turntable position to cover the court as effectively as possible.

Even a player who is not a typical attacker should storm at unpredictable distances, especially if that serves to catch the opponent off guard. The tactical plan (for example, a particularly effective serve or the opponent's recognized weak return or passing shot) is the determining factor in following the serve to the net.

Service to the Center Service Line—Net Play

When the player follows the serve to the center service line, the opponent has no particularly good angle for a passing shot to score a winner. The server should count on a safe return since the opponent will have to stretch less for the return. Moreover, after the return, the opponent is standing in the middle of the court and in an ideal position to defend against a volley. So with this type of net attack (service in the direction of the center service line), the server and the receiver start with about equal chances.

Service to Sideline—Net Play

When a player follows a serve toward the outside and to the net, the opponent has a good angle for a passing ball down the line and to the short cross side. However, to do that, the opponent must run even farther toward the outside or reach farther. Furthermore, after the return, the opponent has opened up the court for the server's volley. Again, servers and receivers theoretically have approximately equal chances—this time for a winner. On dirt courts, the player making the return has a slight advantage since the serve is easier to get to and a volley is harder to put away. On fast courts, on the other hand, the server has an advantage.

First Volley

The first volley is undoubtedly the more important one. A player should go for a direct winner only from a really good shot position.

Normally this first volley, which forces players to hit while running forward, is a preparatory shot played long to the baseline. It should be used to force the opponent into a defensive posture or to compel an imprecise passing ball. After having moved up farther, the player can then score a point on the next volley. When serving, a player should, in all circumstances, attempt to hit the ball effectively as a volley while running forward since hitting a half volley is usually harder than a deep volley.

Attack Ball—Net Play

Balls that bounce at midcourt are often unlucky shots by the opponent (except for the short cross). They should be used in attacking the net.

Here is what a player needs to know to act correctly from a tactical standpoint:

- Where should the attack ball be directed? What is the location of the best turntable position for covering the court after the attack shot?

The answers to these two questions are closely connected to one another.

Best Ready Position for Net Play

Naturally, the ideal position, or the so-called turntable position, theoretically lies along the bisector of the angle of the best-possible returns. Those are a shot down the line, a cross, a short cross, and a lob.

Since no player at the net is in a position to cover a good shot down the line and a short cross equally well, for tactical reasons a certain portion of the court must remain uncovered in order to intercept all other balls. Of course, the player chooses the shot that will create the most problems for the opponent. Without doubt, this is the short cross. This explains why the short cross is not considered in the tactical concept. The positions indicated in figures 54 and 55 are the turntable positions that the player who is charging forward should endeavor to assume. In other words, these positions move the shot position

of an attack ball up to the next point.

Best Direction for an Attack Ball

Depending on where the ball bounces on the court, a player should attack according to the *three-zone theory* (see fig. 58).

If the ball bounces in zone 1 around the service line, a player can attack from point A_1 toward left or right, as desired, since the corresponding turntable positions P_1 and P_2 are equally easy to get to. If the ball bounces in zone 2, an attack down the line becomes viable, based on the shorter running distance from A_2 to P_2. The player should take up the position that is closer and quicker to reach (P_2). If the ball lands in zone 3, the attack down the line may be the only choice, based on the distance from A_3 to P_1 or P_2. This occurs when a ball comes on down the line. However, if it comes on cross court, the ball is better returned cross court at the outer edge of the reach, usually in the doubles court (A_3). To have a good chance at a volley in this instance, a player must first gain some time. That is why the ball is played cross court—it takes longer to get to B_1 than to B_2. In addition, the returned ball comes from the opponent at point B_1 (after the cross attack) fairly straight on. In contrast, after an attack down the line on B_2, playing the dreaded passing shot down the line in the opposite direction of the run is possible. This so-called shot in the back is so difficult to reach because the player has to move very quickly

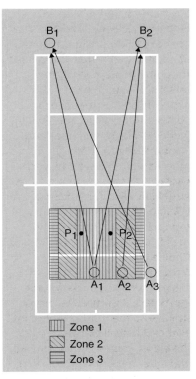

Fig. 58

toward P_2 to have any chance at all against a possible cross passing shot from B_2. Therefore, a crossing shot to B_1, with the longer distance between A_3 and P_1, is better than the attack down the line on B_2, with the shorter distance from A_3 to P_2.

Many players prefer to attack cross court instead of down the line. That depends on whether or not they have a better mastery of the cross shot from midcourt. They may be able to deliver it more aggressively because it is a more dependable shot for them. Also, many opponents find playing a good passing ball down the line from a cross-attack shot to be harder. These direction-changing shots must be hit very cleanly, and that is not easy to do under pressure. In addition, although the ideal shot direction is clear in the theoretical realm, practical exposure to the opponent's abilities and skills is a better guide to which type of attack is more likely to succeed. In other words, even if a player knows that some action is normally called for, unconventionality can sometimes be used for variety in tactics.

Choice of Shot

Topspin, slice, and a straight shot are all appropriate for an attack ball. As usual, the player should use the most reliable shot. With a slow ball (usually a slice), the player comes farther forward into a better position for fielding a volley. At the same time, the opponent has a little more time to come up with a good passing shot.

A fast attack ball forces the participant into a more defensive posture. The player thus takes a position a little farther from the net in starting a volley since the opponent's shot comes back sooner.

Tactics in Doubles

Choice of Partner

Teamwork involves working together to bring a tactical concept to fruition. The partners should get along with one another as well as possible and complement one another's abilities. The basic requirement for success in doubles play is therefore choosing the right partner. The criteria that govern the choice should include these points:

- reciprocal sympathy: the players must understand one another; players who cannot stand each other will never work well together; this surfaces especially in crisis situations, when trust and encouragement become more important than scoring a point right away; trust in the partner's ability and commitment are the basis for a perfect combination;

- similar strengths and a common concept of the game: views on tennis in general and on doubles in particular should coincide;

- different types of players: one sets up plays and the other executes them; one is temperamental and the other calm; one is an artist and the other a craftsman; these types of combinations complement one another well;

- the right positioning on the court: the issue of who plays left or right affects the quality of each partner's returns;

- the right division of labor: who is in charge of the pair? even though both partners have the same rights, one should be in charge; the leader determines who hits the ball in the middle, who runs after the lob, and when to approach the net or back up; leading and accepting leadership in someone else are qualities that not everyone possesses.

Typical positions of players and direction of return (cross) in world-class doubles.

Tactics

Positions and Tasks of the Four Doubles Players

Server

The server stands about 3 or 6 feet (1 to 2 m) to the left or right of the center mark of the baseline (fig. 59, position A). The serve should mainly target the opponent's backhand. A backhand return of a serve from the right is very difficult since only limited room is available for a good backhand shot. The player at the net can therefore concentrate more on the middle since a passing shot down the line is not very likely. The same applies to a serve from the left since the backhand return down the line is likewise a very tricky shot from a technical viewpoint.

When a player serves and follows the shot to the net—which is appropriate on the first and second serves in order to come up to the same level as the partner—the first volley should be placed between the two opponents (according to the midpoint theory). This is especially true when the player has to play a volley from low to high and in response to a good return by the opponent. If the opponent hits a high (or, bad) return, the player can play the return from high to low. That is, the ball can be hit cross court to one side or to the feet of the opponent standing at the net.

The Server's Partner

Normally, this player takes a position in the forward half of the service court opposite the receiving opponent (see fig. 59,

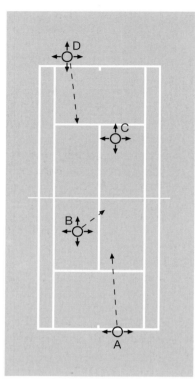

Fig. 59

position B). The better this player can smash or the better the partner can serve, the closer the player can get to the net.

The player at the net should intercept the opponent's return any time that seems feasible. Having the partner run up to the net on the appropriate side can also be arranged beforehand. This go-between move should be attempted, even though it may not always work perfectly, so that the player making the return always has to be wary of an attack. With a serve from the right to the backhand side, the angle for a successful return down the line is very poor. With a serve from the left, the

player's own forehand volley effectively covers the opponent's possible backhand shot down the line.

If the partner hits from the right to the opponent's forehand, moving a little to the left to defend against a possible forehand return down the line, by using a backhand volley, is necessary. The partner's serve from the left to the opponent's forehand side changes the angles for a return to good advantage. If the opponent's cross-court return is always so good that the player at the net cannot attack and the partner cannot volley effectively, the players should try to prevent that exceptionally good backhand shot. To do so, the player has to stand in the other service court across from the backhander's partner in a tandem system. That forces the opponent to make a return down the line, which may be more difficult. Since players always have to deal with lob returns, the partners should clearly understand who is to cover that type of shot. Usually, the player being passed over is responsible for the lob. Only when the server does not come up to the net with the serve—and this should be the exception—can the net player whom the lob has passed over swap sides and let the server take the lob.

The player at the net should always be in motion. That forces the receiver to keep an eye on the ball and the net player, and that makes it harder to make a composed and calculated return.

The Receiver

The receiver stands about 3 feet (1 m) behind the baseline even with the sideline or about 2 feet (0.5 m) closer to the center (fig. 59, position D). Concentrating fully on the task at hand and avoiding getting irritated by the possible moves of the opposing net player are important.

A good return is a short cross directed to the feet of the server who is running forward; the ideal target of the serve is the service line. Topspin is very well suited for that since it makes the ball drop fast once it has crossed the net. In addition, topspin forces the server, who is charging forward, to hit a volley from low to high. However, even a slice can be a very effective return in doubles, especially against very fast and accurate serves that leave no time for a normal baseline shot.

Even some returns down the line and lobs should be thrown in for variety. That will keep the opposing net player from making too many go-betweens.

On a return of a weak second serve, the player should move up a little and make as good a shot as possible. The target should not be the baseline but the feet of the opponent who is running forward. If time is available, the stronger forehand return can be used in preference to the backhand. That needs to be a really good shot, because as the player runs to set up the forehand shot, a portion of the player's own court will be left unprotected. To the extent possible, upon making the return shot, the returner should move up to the net at the same level as the partner for the rally.

The Returner's Partner

The partner stands in front of the service line on the half court to be defended, about 3 feet (1 m) to the side of the center line (fig. 59, position C). If the returning partner makes a good return, the player should move up a step or two and attempt to intercept a possible good cross volley on the part of the server. Possible errors are of no consequence since the volleying server has to worry about having the volley intercepted. That player will attempt to play a riskier game and probably make more mistakes. Not starting to move too soon is important, though. Otherwise, the opponent will play the volley down the line.

If the service and net play of the opponents are so good that no chance to attack presents itself, then the player should take up a position back at the baseline beside the partner and return to the normal ready position at the second serve.

Basic Tips on Tactics

Net Play

Since doubles games are won at the net, partners should assume a better (closer) net position than the opponents. Thus, trying to move forward on service and return is important. A good offense is the best defense. A player about 10 feet (3 m) from the net is in an ideal net position. Even a possible lob should not impede the pressure forward to the net. If necessary, players can run back together and play at the same level.

On a Level with the Partner

A good doubles game is evidenced by the fact that both partners function primarily at the same level on the court. Therefore, partners run forward and back together.

Since players are forced to assume various positions out of the ready position, a player should always endeavor to move up to the level of the partner positioned closer to the net. A net player whose partner cannot manage to come up to the same level on the court may find moving back useful. That should happen only in exceptional cases, though, since doubles can scarcely be won from back court. However, if a situation arises where one player is at the net and the other is forced to play at the baseline, both A and B should play the ball to C (in fig. 60). With a shot to player D, no chance arises for either of them to cover effectively the diagonal that runs between A and B.

Both partners should also stand comparable distances from the sideline. If A or B moves to the left after a forehand cross volley from one position to the other, as designated by B in figure 61, B may have to move farther left to cover a possible shot down the line from player D, who could play right down the middle.

A Safe First Serve

In doubles, that the first serve land in the court is particularly important. That keeps the

opponents from moving up for a return of the second serve and getting up to the net faster. So the first serve should not be hit with full power. It should be more conservative. Good placement is more important than speed. A slightly slower serve also makes moving closer to the net and into a better position for a volley possible.

The return and the first volley must likewise stay in the court. A safe shot at the opponent's feet is preferable to a riskier shot intended to score a point directly.

Varying Returns

Even when the preferred return is a cross-court shot, varying the return is important. Playing some lobs and trying to get some shots down the line past the opposing net player are worthwhile. Even if that leads to no direct points, it keeps the opposing net player from going too far into the middle and intercepting cross returns.

The Theory of the Middle

The area between the two opponents is their weakest spot, whether they are standing at the net or at the baseline. The angle of the returning ball—whether as a volley, half volley, or baseline shot—is limited. An offensive team can therefore safely return over the center of the net and effectively cover the ball as it comes back from the middle.

Sometimes even with well-coordinated teams, difficulties occur in sorting out who is responsible for a shot directed between the two players. Teammates have to work out who is to cover the shot in the middle. It is recommended that

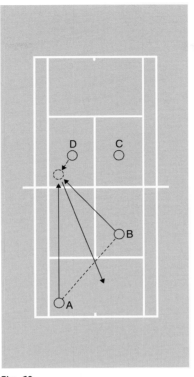

Fig. 60

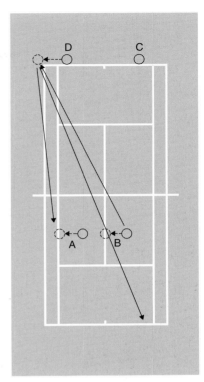

Fig. 61

this be the player stationed on the left (the backhand side) since that player's forehand can be used to cover the middle.

This means that:
- playing the middle against opponents situated at about the same level on the court is best;
- with opponents positioned at different levels on the court, playing the ball to the one farther back is better;
- covering the middle from the opponent's returns by trying to move together to the side and forward or back in the direction of the shot is important.

Flexible Net Play

Net players should always be *on the move*, that is, in motion and not rooted to any spot near the net. Doing so allows the players to react better if the ball is played directly to them or if they want to intercept a return. Additionally, net players who continually move can distract the opponents and keep them from concentrating exclusively on the return. *Going between* (intercepting returns)—which has to be arranged with the partner—*feinting* (a feigned attack on a return), and the restless behavior of the net player that can undermine the opponent's confidence, should be compulsory exercises for doubles players.

Technique

Toward a Terminology of Stroke Technique

As tennis has developed as a sport, it has been accompanied by a diversification of stroke (shot) techniques. Not surprisingly, tennis literature contains not only a number of shot techniques but also some inconsistent definitions:

- Terminology among books often varies or is unclear.
- Individual terms such as *slice* are used in different ways. As a result, *forehand slice* and *backhand slice* are used to designate shots where backspin is imparted to the ball and *slice service* when the ball is given primarily sidespin.
- Different labels are added to techniques to make them understandable. The term *drive,* for example, is used to imply that fast balls are employed to place the opponent under pressure; *topspin* means that the ball has a pronounced forward spin; the term *volley* is used for a ball hit before it contacts the ground; and

smash indicates not only the spatial position when the ball is hit but also the use of force in making the hit.
- Many technical terms are also provided with additional clarifications to make them more precise; an example is the forehand volley drop shot using the wrist or with a firm wrist.

The designation of techniques is based on the following six characteristics:

1. Spatial position of the player (for example, in service and volley).
2. Point of contact with the ball with reference to the player's body (for example, in forehand and backhand shots).
3. Intended placement of the ball (for example, with drop shots).
4. Rotational behavior of the ball (for example, with topspin shots).
5. Trajectory of the ball to be hit (for example, with a lob).
6. How the move is carried out with reference to the stroke and follow-through phases (for example, a chip shot).

Theoretically, if one were to make the terminology consistent, he or she might have to start with a combination of the primary existing definitions and the needed ones in order to come up with some entirely new ones. The relevant considerations include the following:

- where the ball is hit with respect to the player (on the right or left side, over the top of the head, overhead to the left, and so on);
- the contact point with the ball in relation to where it lands in the court (for example, directly with no contact, immediately after contact, or a brief instant after contact);
- the goal of the shot with reference to where the ball lands in the opposing court (long, medium, or short);
- the goal with reference to the direction of the ball to be hit (for example, straight or angling right or left);
- the goal with reference to the ball's rotation (heavy or mild topspin, backspin, or sidespin);
- the goal with reference to the ball's trajectory (low, high, or very high);
- special conditions (including a ball hit under extreme conditions such as behind the body and to one side).

Combining all these requirements would, however, greatly expand the number of techniques that already exist and make them no more comprehensible. Since technique should be regarded as a purposeful form of movement to accomplish a task, many techniques of addressing conditions already exist or are desired based on the variety of given possibilities. The terms already in use will probably not change. As a result, despite the foregoing observations, the usual terms will be used throughout the remainder of this book.

A Description of Stroke Techniques

Analyzing and describing individual stroke techniques is based on the basic theories of movement, especially *the concept of functional movement analysis*. It involves the following four steps, which, in turn, are comprised of various individual parts:

1. In which situations and from which positions the technique is applied is determined first (for example, a ground shot from near the baseline). This addresses such material conditions as court size, height of net, and other dimensions such as reach. Then the question arises concerning which tactical goals the technique can be successfully applied to in this situation. Next, based on laws of physics, how the ball can be expected to fly and accomplish its tactical purpose can be deduced (for example, with mild topspin and fairly high speed).

2. The conditions that bear on the player's actions can then be considered. In other words, what must the player do to achieve the desired ball trajectory, and for what is the technique used? The next considerations are the distinguishing features of the main action within the stroke phase since they affect the desired ball trajectory according to biomechanical laws. One must then consider the supporting actions that reinforce the main action within the backswing and stroke phases and that demonstrate the correctness of the main action in the follow-through phase.

3. The next step will examine the possible variations that exist in performing various movements and their attendant advantages and disadvantages. This involves the supporting actions in the backswing, stroke, and follow-through phases.

4. Finally, where that leeway crosses the line into the realm of defects and errors will be discussed. The main action will be referred to again when dealing with mistakes.

For a practical application of tennis instruction, considering the following points is useful:

- every technique is presented with the aid of a diagram;
- in the interest of completeness, many descriptions and reasons appear repeatedly with individual steps;
- for reasons of space, only the essential characteristics and illustrations can be included;
- all techniques apply to right-handed players; left-handed players need to reverse the techniques accordingly;
- note that the illustrations present *an average way to perform a movement;* they do not take into account any possible leeway based on individual style; these average movements constitute an ideal for tennis trainers, coaches, and teachers; they should be demonstrated especially when dealing with beginners and should form the basis for instruction and correction; individual learners can then be permitted to exercise a little latitude and deviate from the average performance based on their personal requirements and abilities.

Readers should also keep in mind that from among the various techniques applicable to individual situations, positions, and tactical goals, only one has been chosen for the illustrations. In addition, the ball has usually been played at a moderate speed.

BASIC TECHNIQUES

Ground Stroke— Forehand and Backhand

In what situations and for what purposes is this technique used? What is the ball's trajectory like?

Situations and Positions

Ground shots with forehand and backhand are usually hit near the baseline.

Tactical Goals

- The ball must be kept safely in play.
- The ball should be hit in such a way that it bounces about 6 to 9 feet (2 to 3 m) in front of the opposing baseline and forces the opposing player to stay behind the baseline and return the ball from that area.
- The opponent should be kept under pressure by well-placed and fairly fast shots; this can also serve as a means of setting up an attack at the net.
- In case of a net attack by the opponent, this technique can be used for a passing shot down the line.

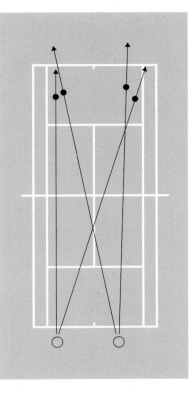

Effects on the Behavior of the Ball

- The ball may fly through the air with mild topspin and a reasonably flat trajectory.
- The ball may travel at a relatively high speed (except to keep the ball in play).

Fig. 62   Aiming points.

Fig. 63   The ball's flight.

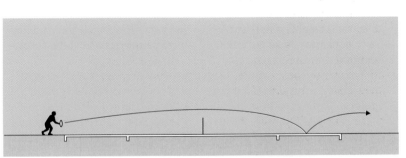

Fig. 64

Ground Stroke— Forehand

What does the player do on a forehand ground stroke in order to achieve the desired trajectory? What is this technique used for?

Features of the Main Action Within the Stroke Phase

- The racket is swung forward and slightly upward (illustrations 7 and 8) to give the ball a little topspin.
- The racket is accelerated to impart the desired velocity to the ball.
- The racket is swung far in the direction of the stroke (illustrations 6–8) to achieve greater accuracy and dependability.
- To achieve the best possible transfer of energy, the ball is hit the proper distance to the side and in front of the body while keeping the racket face vertical.
- Just before contact, the wrist is brought into a position that corresponds to the departure velocity to produce the greatest degree of accuracy.
- Upon contact, the grip on the racket is tightened, and the wrist is held firmly for an instant to provide resistance to the ball.

Features of Supporting Actions

Backswing

- The racket is held with a forehand grip so that the racket face can be held vertically at contact.
- The upper body and the right foot are turned to the right (illustration 2); the racket is held high and back (illustrations 2–4) to provide a fluid transition to the stroke phase (illustrations 4–6).
- The knees are bent.
- The left leg points forward in a closed stance in the anticipated direction of the shot (illustration 4); at that point, the feet should be about hip width apart to help maintain balance.

Stroke Phase

- In the transition to the stroke phase, the racket is positioned under the predictable contact point with the ball (illustrations 5 and 6) so it can be swung forward and upward in the main action.
- For a forehand ground stroke from a closed position, the body weight shifts onto the forward foot (illustrations 5 and 7), and the upper body turns in the direction of the shot when the racket makes contact (illustrations 7 and 8); this rotation of the upper body helps in accelerating the racket.
- The legs begin to straighten to support the upward movement.
- In principle, the right arm remains slightly bent (illustrations 8–10); at greater stroke speeds, it bends even further.

Follow-through Phase

- The racket continues to swing forward and upward in the direction of the shot (illustrations 9–12).
- The legs continue to straighten.

Possible Variations and Their Advantages and Disadvantages

Backswing

- Many players are satisfied simply to take the racket back in a low arc (as in fig. 65); doing this saves time and makes for a precise movement.
- Many players begin the take back with a low arc; this produces a fluid movement and quick acceleration in the stroke phase.
- Often the stroke stance varies according to the situation; the more open it is, the quicker the stroke movement and the more the shot direction tends to cross. However, the shot is often less accurate.
- This movement can vary among individuals in terms of its *timing and dynamics*, especially with respect to the transition between taking the racket back in the backswing phase and accelerating it in the stroke phase.

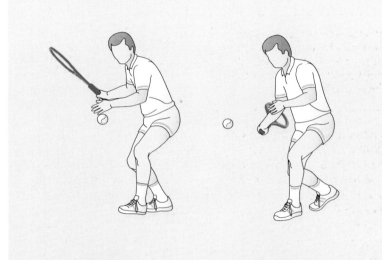

Fig. 65   Backswing with a low, upward arc.

Stroke Phase

- The upper body can be twisted more or less dynamically. That affects the acceleration of the racket.
- The initial speed and the acceleration of the racket in the stroke movement can be accomplished in different ways. The smoother the acceleration of the racket to the contact point with the ball, the safer and more controlled the hit.

Follow-through

- The greater the speed of the racket, the *longer* and higher the follow-through. Some players end the swing above their left shoulder.

Common Flaws and Mistakes

Backswing

- When using the *semicontinental grip,* the transfer of force is less than optimal; difficulties increase at higher contact points.
- Using the *backhand grip* makes keeping the racket face vertical at the desired contact point difficult.
- *Little or no upper-body rotation* interferes with adequate take back of the racket; as a result, accelerating the racket adequately becomes difficult and it leads to a punching movement rather than to a swing in the stroke phase.
- A *very late backswing* reduces the chance of hitting the ball at the right moment and under control.
- Using an *exaggerated or very high backswing* creates the danger that the ball may be hit too late at the expense of accuracy.
- A *noticeable pause* at the end of the backswing interferes with the flow of the movement and contributes to a sudden acceleration of the racket.

Stroke Phase

- *Failure to lower the racket head below the anticipated contact point* makes swinging

Fig. 66   Leaning back during the shot.

Fig. 67   Turning too early in the direction of the shot.

the racket in a forward and upward motion impossible.
- *Straightening the legs too early* mostly detracts from coordination.
- *Leaning back* interferes with the desirable weight shift forward and upward, which, in turn, detracts from acceleration and can spoil the shot (see fig. 66).
- *Turning the hips and upper body too early* creates poor coordination between body rotation and arm swing and produces a stroke that lacks rhythm and control (see fig. 67).
- When using an *inappropriate contact point* (that is, too late, too close, and too far from the body), safety and precision suffer greatly.

- A *limp wrist at the moment of contact* greatly detracts from control.

Follow-through

- *Ending the follow-through too early* by stopping the stroke movement greatly interferes with control.
- *Changing the natural follow-through direction* too early by turning the forearm (that is, a pronation movement) or by bending the wrist or the elbow shortly after contact has a very negative impact on ball control.

Fig. 68

Ground Stroke—Backhand

What does the player do in a backhand ground stroke to produce the desired ball trajectory? What is this technique used for?

Features of the Main Action Within the Stroke Phase

- The racket is swung forward and slightly upward to give the ball some topspin.
- The racket is accelerated to produce the desired ball velocity.
- The racket is swung far in the direction of the shot (illustrations 7–9) to produce greater accuracy and safety.
- The ball is hit with a vertical racket face the right distance to the side and a little farther in front of the body than with a forehand shot (illustration 9); this produces an ideal transfer of energy.
- Just before contact, the wrist is brought into a position appropriate to the ball's departure velocity to create to the greatest degree of accuracy.
- Upon contact, the grip on the racket is tightened and the wrist is held firmly for a brief moment to provide some resistance to the ball.

Features of Supporting Actions

Backswing

- The racket is held with a backhand grip so that the racket face can be held vertically at contact.
- The upper body is turned back sharply and assumes a pronounced lateral position.
- At the same time, the left hand guides the racket back by holding it at the throat (illustration 3) to stabilize the backswing and to aid in turning the upper body further.
- The right foot steps forward so that the right half of the back points toward the net (illustration 5); this aids in the subsequent acceleration by the arm in the direction of the shot.

- The racket is taken back and upward; this arc is *straighter* than with the forehand ground stroke.
- The knees are bent.

Stroke Phase

- With reference to the anticipated contact point, the racket head is lowered during the transition to the stroke phase (illustrations 5, 6, and 7) so that it can be swung forward and upward in the main action.
- To maintain balance, the feet should be at least hip width apart (illustration 8).
- To support the acceleration of the racket, the body weight should be shifted strongly onto the forward leg at the start of the stroke phase; this weight shift takes place earlier than with a forehand stroke, and the upper body is turned only to the point where the axis of the shoulders points in the direction of the shot (illustrations 8 and 9).

- The lateral position of the feet and body is maintained right through the moment of contact (illustrations 9–11) to facilitate the best possible hit.
- Before contact, the right arm is straightened (illustrations 7 and 8) to set up an optimal contact point and energy transfer.

Follow-through

- The swing of the racket is continued in the direction of the shot (illustrations 10–12). At the end of the follow-through, the racket and right side of the body point in the direction of the shot (illustration 12).

Possible Variations and Their Advantages and Disadvantages

Backswing

- Many players are content to hit using the *semicontinental grip;* this might be easier, but it is less than ideal in transferring energy, and the ball is not hit at a point far enough from the body.
- Many players start the backswing with a downward arc; this may help in creating a more fluid swing, but it may also keep the player from getting into the stroke phase at the right instant from the lower arc of the loop.
- *Lack of support from the left hand in the backswing* is common; often the upper body is not twisted far enough to the rear.
- Controlling the movement is harder, especially the transition between the backswing and stroke phases.
- The *timing and dynamics* of this movement can vary among individuals, especially in the transition between the take back of the racket and its acceleration in the stroke phase.

Stroke Phase

- The arm can be straightened at the start of the stroke phase or just before the main action.

Follow-through

- The greater the desired racket speed, the *longer* the follow-through.
- At high stroke speeds, the racket swings *steeply upward and to the right,* and the upper body turns in the direction of the shot.

Common Flaws and Mistakes

Backswing

- Using the *forehand grip* makes keeping the racket face vertical at the desired contact point very hard and reduces the transfer of force.
- Using *little or no twist in the upper body and a very short backswing* interferes with racket acceleration and often produces a punching movement in the stroke phase.

- A *late backswing* reduces the chances of hitting the ball at the right moment and leads to an uncontrolled swing.
- An *excessively wide take back with a straight arm* interferes with swing and coordination.

Stroke Phase

- *Failure to keep the shoulder to the side* often interferes with swinging the arm in the desired direction.
- *Failure to lower the racket head* below the anticipated contact point means swinging the racket forward and upward is not possible.
- *Straightening the legs too soon* mainly interferes with coordination (see fig. 69).
- *Leaning back* detracts from racket acceleration and leads to lack of control at contact.
- When *the lateral stance is abandoned too soon*, the whole body rotates in the stroke movement; this significantly detracts from ball control (see fig. 70).
- Using an *awkward contact point*, in other words, too late, too close, or too far from the body (see fig. 71), detracts from acceleration and reduces control.
- A *failure to straighten the arm* when the ball is hit indicates that the racket swing has been checked and that the contact point is too close to the side of the body.

Follow-through

- *Ending the follow-through too early* by checking the swing movement.
- *Deviating from the direction of the shot too early* interferes with ball control as do other errors.
- *Strong and excessive bending in the wrist* indicates that the swing was checked too early to the detriment of the energy transfer (see fig. 72).

Fig. 71 Awkward, late contact point.

Fig. 69 Straightening the legs too soon.

Fig. 70 Abandoning the lateral stroke position too early.

Fig. 72 Exaggerated bend in wrist.

Two-handed Backhand

In what situations and for what purposes is this technique applied? What is the ball's trajectory like?

Situations and Positions
- The two-handed backhand is usually used to hit the ball after it bounces near the baseline.

Tactical Goals
- The ball must be kept in play.
- The ball should be hit in such a way that it bounces about 6 to 10 feet (2 to 3 m) in front of the baseline, forcing the opponent to remain behind the baseline and return the ball from that area.
- A well-placed and fairly fast ball should put the pressure onto the opponent; this can also set up an attack at the net.
- This technique can also be used for a passing shot, especially down the line, when the opponent is attacking at the net.

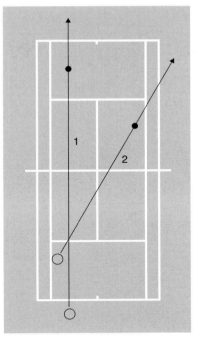

Effects on the Behavior of the Ball
- In general, the ball should be played at a fairly high speed.
- Depending on the tactical goal, the ball may fly fast and low or slower, higher, and farther.

Fig. 73   Aiming points (*left*).

Fig. 74   Flight of ball (*below*).

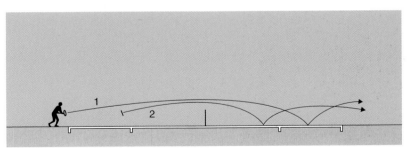

With a two-handed backhand, the right upper arm is close to the body, and the left shoulder moves sharply forward and upward.

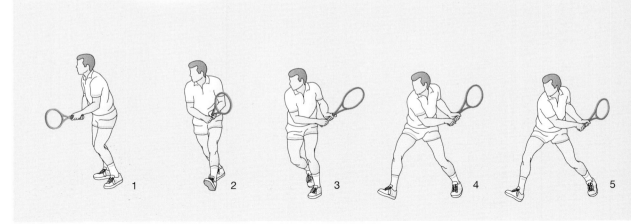

Fig. 75

What does the player do in a two-handed backhand to produce the desired ball trajectory? What is this technique used for?

Features of the Main Action Within the Stroke Phase

- The racket is swung forward and slightly upward to give the ball slight topspin.
- The racket is accelerated to achieve the right velocity at the moment of contact.
- The ball is hit to the side of and at an appropriate distance from the body using a vertical racket face (illustration 8); this increases ball control and facilitates energy transfer.
- Just before contact with the ball, the wrists are positioned to impart to the ball the appropriate velocity and accuracy.
- Upon contact, the grip is tightened, and the wrists are held firmly for an instant to provide resistance to the ball.

Features of Supporting Actions

Backswing

- The racket is held with both hands so that the racket face can be held vertically at contact. The right hand can use a backhand grip.
- The upper body is turned back sharply (with the right half of the back pointing toward the net) to provide adequate room for the backswing (illustrations 2 and 3); at the turning point, the right arm is nearly straight, and the left one is bent (illustration 6).
- Because of the two-handed hold, the racket follows a relatively flat arc as it is swung in a loop (illustrations 1–4).
- During the backswing, the right leg moves forward at an angle toward the oncoming ball.
- The knees are bent (illustrations 3–6).

Stroke Phase

- In the transition to the stroke phase, the head of the racket is placed lower than the anticipated contact point so that during the stroke phase, it can be swung upward as well as forward.
- At the start of the stroke movement, the right foot is placed in the direction of the oncoming ball at least a shoulder's width in front of the left foot; during the stroke phase, the body weight is transferred to the right foot (illustration 5).
- Because of the two-handed grip, the upper body must rotate in the direction of the shot (illustrations 6–8); this helps with acceleration.
- During the stroke phase, the arms remain slightly bent; at higher stroke speeds, they are bent more.
- The right hand helps in the energy transfer; the major part of the swing usually comes from body rotation and the left arm.

Follow-through
- The racket continues to swing in the direction of the shot (illustrations 9 and 10).

Possible Variations and Their Advantages and Disadvantages

Backswing
- Many players assume an open stance in the backswing phase; the upper body rotation tenses their muscles quite effectively, providing better racket acceleration during the shot.
- The follow-through often follows a straight line rearward and downward; this stroke movement rarely places the player under any time pressure.
- In the backswing, the wrist is often bent; this makes taking the racket head farther back and accelerating quickly in the stroke movement possible.

Stroke Phase
- With shots made from a lateral stance, particularly with fast stroke movements, the left leg is moved ahead in the direction of the shot to maintain balance.
- Both arms can remain more or less bent since this improves control.
- During the stroke movement, the left shoulder moves sharply forward and upward; the right upper arm is held close to the body. This configuration is particularly advantageous with relatively high contact points.

Follow-through
- Many players *release the left hand from the racket* upon contact and complete the swing with only the right hand.
- *The follow-through occurs quickly over the right shoulder.*

Common Flaws and Mistakes

Backswing
- *Too little upper body rotation* makes for an excessively short backswing. The result is too little swing, and the ball is punched.
- *If the right arm is not brought back far enough and is too far away from the body,* it restricts the swing in the stroke phase.

Stroke Phase
- *Straightening the legs too soon* is especially detrimental to coordination.
- *Improper contact points* detract from reliability and precision.

Follow-through
- *Stopping the follow-through too early* by checking the swing has a very negative effect on ball control.

Volley— Forehand and Backhand

In what situations and for what purposes is this technique used? What is the ball trajectory like?

Situations and Positions

- The forehand and backhand volley are usually used in the area between midcourt and the net (ideally 6 to 10 feet [2 to 3 m] in front of the net).

Tactical Goals

- The ball should travel to a spot as close as possible to the opposing baseline, especially when it is hit near the service line. This places the opponent under pressure and gives the player enough time to take up a favorable position at the net (see both figures, #1).
- The ball should be played in such a way that the opponent is forced far out of the court to one side or can not reach the ball. This works especially well when the volley is played close to the net (see both figures, #2).

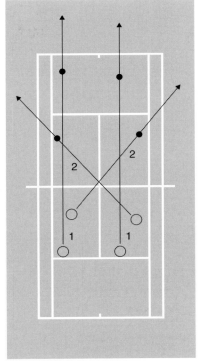

Fig. 76 Aiming points.

Fig. 77 Flight of ball.

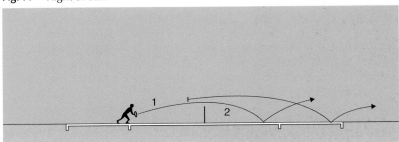

- Fast shots put pressure onto the opponent and provoke hasty, uncontrolled shots.
- In volley play, the opponent should have no time to get into a good position on the court after making a shot. A player can end the rally by making an unreachable shot contrary to the opponent's running direction or into a distant corner of the court.
- The foregoing goals notwithstanding, the ball should be played fairly safely.

Effects on the Behavior of the Ball

- The ball may travel quite fast.
- The ball may be hit with backspin.

Fig. 78

Volley—Forehand

What does the player do in a forehand volley to achieve the desired ball trajectory? What is this technique used for?

Features of the Main Action Within the Stroke Phase

- The racket is swung forward and slightly downward to give the ball backspin.
- The racket is accelerated up to the contact point to hit the ball as soon as possible and give it the desired velocity.
- The ball is hit to the side and in front of the body to transfer energy as effectively as possible. At that point, the racket face is vertical or slightly open above the net (illustration 7); with a low contact point, it is open.
- Just before contact, the wrist is brought into a position that corresponds to the departure velocity to create the highest degree of accuracy.

- At contact, the grip is tightened, and the wrist is held firmly for a brief instant to provide resistance to the ball.

Features of Supporting Actions

Backswing

- The racket is held with the forehand grip so that the racket face can be held nearly vertically at contact and the ball can be hit in front of the body.
- The upper body is rotated back and the forearm is raised so that the racket head rises above the anticipated contact point (illustrations 2 and 3); this allows a swing in a forward and downward direction.
- In so doing, the racket is taken back only a short distance behind the right shoulder (illustration 5). For reasons of time, this makes for a shorter backswing than with ground shots.
- Body weight is shifted onto the right leg (illustration 2). For

volleys with a low contact point, *the left foot is planted before the stroke movement begins;* the player needs no support from weight transfer in the stroke because a low volley is not played so forcefully and the player is better balanced. For volleys with a contact point higher than the net, the left leg does not move forward in that way; rather, it is used to take a step toward the ball during the swing.

Stroke Phase

- During the stroke movement directed forward and downward, the elbow is gradually straightened (illustrations 4–7); this sets up an ideal contact point.
- Simultaneously with the arm movement, the left leg takes a step to meet the ball (illustrations 3–6); this weight transfer forward and downward supports the stroke.

As the left foot is placed onto the court surface, the leg bends (illustrations 6 and 7) to support the forward and downward movement.

The upper body turns in the direction of the shot (illustrations 5–7); this helps in contacting the ball early.

Follow-through

In the follow-through, the movement continues further forward and downward in the direction of the shot and finishes in a slight movement directed forward and upward that flows smoothly into the starting position (illustrations 8–10).

Possible Variations and Their Advantages and Disadvantages

Backswing

Many players use the *semicontinental grip;* when a player uses this grip with a backhand volley, the grip does not have to change. A disadvantage is that the transfer of force is less effective; when the racket face is held vertically, the contact point is not far enough forward, and a lot of wrist action is required. With the semicontinental grip, hitting the ball on a low volley with a more open racket face is easier.

For slow oncoming balls, the racket can be taken *farther back;* at the end of the backswing, the stroke arm is nearly straight. This sets up a longer acceleration path and makes hitting the ball harder and farther into the opposing court possible.

Many players take the racket back in a straight line, and in the transition to the stroke phase, they raise it higher than the anticipated contact point (in a reverse loop); this creates an advantage especially with high contact points.

Stroke Phase

Many players maintain a constant angle in the elbow. This can adversely affect control of shots down the line, but it reduces undesirable punching motions.

With slow oncoming balls, the swing can be *more sweeping;* this can, however, detract somewhat from shot control.

With fast oncoming balls, the *stroke is very short,* and the ball is almost blocked; more extensive movement would lead to hitting the ball too late and unreliably.

Follow-through

The follow-through varies considerably according to the dynamics of the shot; still, the transition into the starting position is fairly fluid.

Fig. 79 Very high and extended back-swing in a forehand volley.

Fig. 80 Hitting the ball too late in a forehand volley.

Fig. 81 Premature weight transfer in a forehand volley.

Common Flaws and Mistakes

Backswing

- Using the *backhand grip* inter-feres with optimal transfer of force; the contact point lies too far to the rear; and the racket face is seldom vertical.
- With a *very high and extended backswing,* the stroke is not made in the desired forward direction but, rather, in front of the body and toward the left (see fig. 79).
- In a backswing with completely straight arm, the direction of the stroke movement tends more toward the left front of the body, and the ball often picks up sidespin.

Stroke Phase

- The *stroke is not directed forward and downward;* consequently there is no control or reliability.
- *Exaggeration of the downward movement* will produce lots of backspin, but the ball picks up only minimal speed.
- In the stroke movement, the arm straightens at the elbow away from the body (in a punching movement). This detracts from ball speed and control.
- *Hitting the ball too late* makes weight transfer impossible (see fig. 80).
- Having a *loose grip* when the ball is hit adversely affects ball control and safety.

- With *late or nonexistent weight transfer,* the movement is performed with only the arm; coordination among move-ments and ball control are lacking (see fig. 81).

Follow-through

- *Starting the follow-through too early* forward and upward greatly reduces ball control in the volley.

Footwork and stroke movement are very well coordinated.

Fig. 82

Volley—Backhand

What does the player do in a backhand volley to achieve the desired ball trajectory? What is this technique used for?

Features of the Main Action Within the Stroke Phase

- The racket is swung forward and slightly downward to give the ball backspin.
- The racket is accelerated up to the contact point to achieve the desired velocity and to hit the ball as early as possible.
- The ball is hit at the side and in front of the body to effect the best-possible energy transfer. With a contact point higher than the net, the racket face is nearly vertical at contact (illustration 7); with a low contact point, it is open.
- Just before contact, the wrist is brought into a position

that corresponds to the departure velocity and creates the greatest degree of accuracy.
- The grip is tightened at contact, and the wrist is held firmly for a brief instant to provide resistance to the ball.

Features of Supporting Actions

Backswing

- The racket is held with a backhand grip so that the racket face can be held nearly vertically at contact and the ball can be hit in front of the body.
- The upper body is rotated back so that the axis of the shoulders is parallel to the direction of the shot and the forearm is slightly raised (illustrations 2 and 3); this facilitates a stroke in a forward and downward direction.
- The racket is taken back only a little behind the left shoulder (illustration 4). This makes for a considerably

shorter backswing than with a ground shot.
- During the backswing, the left hand remains on the throat of the racket and helps in rotating the upper body (illustrations 2 and 3).
- Body weight shifts to the left leg. On a volley with a low contact point, the right foot is planted before the stroke; but with a high contact point, it is not planted before contact so that the player can take a step to meet the ball.

Stroke Phase

- The elbow is straightened in the course of the forward and downward stroke (illustrations 4–6) to create the desired racket acceleration and an early contact point.
- At the start of the stroke, the player steps toward the ball with the right foot (illustrations 4–6); this weight transfer contributes to the stroke.

- The right leg bends as the foot is planted onto the court (illustrations 5 and 6); this contributes to the forward and downward movement.
- The shoulder remains parallel to the shot direction (illustrations 6 and 7), providing adequate control and great accuracy.
- The left arm moves slightly to the rear to aid in maintaining balance and preserving the lateral stroke position (illustrations 6 and 7).

Follow-through

- In the follow-through, the stroke continues in a forward and downward direction and ends with a slight movement upward and forward (illustrations 8–10) that flows smoothly into the starting position.
- The left arm moves farther away from the body to help maintain balance.

Possible Variations and Their Advantages and Disadvantages

Backswing

- For a backhand volley, many players hold the racket with a *semicontinental grip;* this grip is suited to playing low volleys. For balls hit at greater than net height, keeping the racket face vertical at contact is difficult, and the transfer of energy is not very effective.
- With high contact points (at shoulder height and above), the upper arm and forearm are nearly parallel to the ground; *the elbow is at about shoulder height,* and the racket head may be a bit lower.
- Some players keep their arm long in the backswing; this helps control the distance to the contact point.

Stroke Phase

- For a slow oncoming ball, the stroke movement can be *more sweeping;* this lets the player accelerate the ball without using an undue amount of energy.
- With high contact points, the stroke begins by raising the racket head by *pivoting the forearm* around the elbow joint. The momentum brings the racket head above the anticipated contact point.
- With a very fast oncoming ball, the stroke is *shortened considerably* in order to hit the ball at the right moment.

Follow-through

- The follow-through *varies considerably according to the dynamics of the shot.* It may be entirely eliminated in extreme cases, but the transition into the starting position should be fairly fluid.

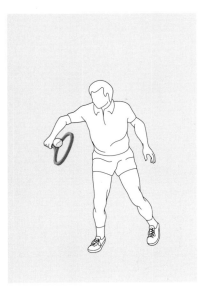

Fig. 83 Bent arm in hitting backhand volley (left).

Fig. 84 Rotating the upper body too early in a backhand volley.

Common Flaws and Mistakes

Backswing

- Using the *forehand grip* interferes with energy transfer, and the contact point is too far to the rear.
- If *the upper body is rotated too little or not at all,* the contact point will be too close to the body and the stroke will veer too far to the right.
- When *the elbow points in the direction of the shot,* this produces a shot from only the forearm (a punching motion).

Stroke Phase

- When the *stroke is not directed forward and downward,* reliability and control are lacking.
- *Exaggeration of downward motion* will produce lots of backspin, but it will not give the ball much speed.
- When the *arm remains bent during the stroke,* this produces a movement to the right rather than in the desired forward direction; the ball picks up sidespin (see fig. 83).
- *Rotating the upper body too soon and too much* has an adverse effect on accuracy and control (see fig. 84).
- *Hitting the ball too late* makes weight transfer impossible.

- A *loose grip when the ball is hit* significantly detracts from ball control and safety.
- By using *too-early or nonexistent weight transfer,* in this case, if the movement is made with only the arm, coordination among movements and ball control are lacking.

Follow-through

- *Starting the follow-through too early* forward and upward greatly reduces ball control.

The stroke arm straightens before contact.

Serve

In what situations and for what purposes is this technique used? What is the ball trajectory like?

Situations and Positions

- The serve is hit as an opening shot from behind the baseline and according to the score, from left or right of the center mark.

Tactical Goals

- The ball is to be hit into the service court diagonally opposite the server.
- With the first serve, the player should attempt to score a point directly or put pressure onto

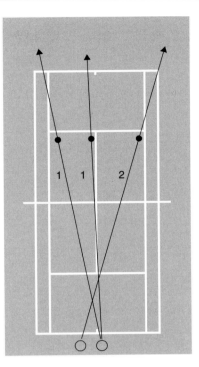

the opponent through speed and ball placement, thereby forcing a weak or faulty return.
- The second serve should be played primarily with a view to safety and placement since a failed serve would constitute a double fault and a lost point.
- Generally, the second serve should be played to the opponent's weaker return side.

Effects on the Behavior of the Ball

- On the first serve, the ball should travel at a high speed and in a flat curve (1).
- On the second serve, the ball should cross the net at a lower speed in a pronounced arc (2).

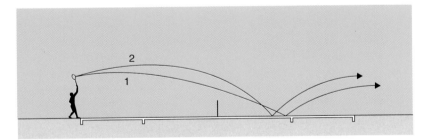

Fig. 85 Aiming points (*above*).

Fig. 86 Ball flight (*below*).

Fig. 87

Features of the Main Action Within the Stroke Phase

- The racket head is accelerated to the maximum in an upward and forward motion (illustrations 8–11) until it contacts the ball.
- At contact, the racket head is practically vertical to the ground and at right angles to the direction of the shot.
- Pronation of the arm just before contact turns the racket face at a right angle to the direction of the shot (illustrations 10 and 11).
- The ball is hit at its highest point about 8 inches (20 cm) in front of the left foot and the baseline (illustration 11).

Features of Supporting Actions

- The racket is held with the backhand or semicontinental grip.
- Feet are placed about shoulder width apart (illustration 1) to provide a stable starting position.
- At the start of the backswing phase, the racket is swung pendulum-like in a low downward and upward arc (illustrations 1–3).
- The upper body turns (illustrations 3–5), and the body weight simultaneously transfers briefly to the right leg (illustrations 1–3).
- During the pendulum movement with the racket, the left arm straightens to toss the ball into the air; the wrist is kept straight (illustrations 1–3).
- The throwing arm is raised in the direction of the right net post so that the ball can be thrown to the best contact point.

- The ball leaves the hand at about forehead level (illustration 3); this aids in controlling the height and direction of the toss.
- The ball is tossed slightly above the highest contact point that can be reached with the racket.
- The shoulder axis inclines increasingly rearward and downward (illustrations 3–5).
- Simultaneously with the weight transfer to the left foot, the upper body bends back, the pelvis thrusts forward, and the left knee in particular bends (illustrations 4 and 5).
- The upper body inclines farther rearward to complete bending the bow; this tension facilitates a long acceleration path.
- As the knees and pelvis thrust forward, the racket is brought to a point over the right shoulder by bending the elbow (illustrations 4 and 5).

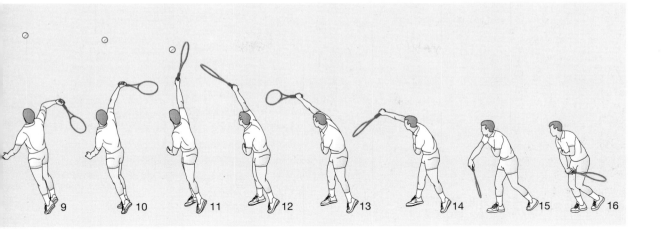

Stroke Phase

- Up to the contact point, the body straightens from low to high; the knees are the first to straighten (illustrations 6–8).
- The muscles of the hips, abdomen, chest, and shoulders then contract in succession (illustrations 7–9), and finally the wrist is brought into play (illustration 11).
- As a result of dynamic straightening, jumping off the left foot commonly occurs.
- The racket is at the lowest point in the loop behind the back when the knees are completely straight.
- At the start of the serve, the left arm lowers.
- As the body straightens (thereby releasing the tension in the bow), the upper body turns in the direction of the shot (illustrations 8–11).
- The racket accelerates up to the contact point.
- At contact, the shoulder of the striking arm is as high as possible. The arm is completely straight. The left foot, right shoulder, and right hand are perpendicular to the ground. The left arm is held in front of the body for stability.

Follow-through

- After contact, the right forearm rotates farther inward (pronation) and swings to the right (illustrations 12 and 13).
- Because of the great acceleration of the racket in the main action and the pronation of the arm, the wrist tips forward and to the right at the end of the stroke (illustration 14).
- The upper body follows the ball in the direction of the shot.
- The right arm swings in front of the body and to the left side (illustration 16).
- The left arm remains in front of the body (illustrations 11–16).
- After jumping off the left foot, the landing is likewise usually done on the left foot. In the absence of a jump, the right foot supports the body weight.

Possible Variations and Their Advantages and Disadvantages

Backswing

- Differences occur in *how the ball toss and the movement of the racket are coordinated:*
  - both arms can be lowered and raised simultaneously
  - the upward movement of the ball hand can be relatively quick and short
  - the racket arm can be moved downward and the ball arm raised

All three means can produce a good serve. Depending on how the various individual movements are strung together, they affect how high the ball is tossed.

- Many players prefer a short backswing, using no pendulum movement; this helps them with coordination and timing.
- Many players toss the ball up with a *slight bend in their arm.* However, keeping the arm straight helps retain better control over the height and direction of the toss.

- Many players begin the serve *with their weight on the right foot.* In so doing, guarding against straightening the knees too early in the weight transfer to the left foot is important.
- Rotating the upper body, tensing the elbow, and bending the knees can be done to different degrees.

Stroke Phase
- Timing and dynamics in the stroke phase can vary significantly among individuals.
- *Use of the body* (straightening the knees and rotating the upper body) in support of racket acceleration can vary significantly among different players.
- Most players *jump up* from the left foot and land on the same foot when playing hard.

Follow-through
- *The landing* can involve either the right or the left leg.
- *The follow-through ends in front of the body.*

Common Flaws and Mistakes

Backswing
- When using the *forehand grip,* the ball cannot be hit at the highest possible point.
- An excessively high swing with the racket arm (with the forearm vertical to the ground) causes the movement of the racket to come from only the elbow.

- When using an *exaggerated frontal body position* and lack of upper-body rotation in backswing, the serve comes from only arm movement.
- Failure to bend the knees interferes with motion transfer from low to high.
- *Drawing the upper arm into the torso* by bending the elbow interrupts the flow of the movement and reduces acceleration (see fig. 88).
- *Straightening the body too soon* (see fig. 89) means the body is not being used properly, and this leads to tilting the upper body forward before making contact.
- *Failure to toss the ball high enough* leads to a hasty backswing, and the body is not fully extended when the ball is hit.
- *Tossing the ball too far forward, to the side, or to the rear* means the ball is not hit at the optimal contact point, greatly hindering control.

Stroke Phase
- *Interrupting the flow of the movement* at the lowest point of the loop interferes with maximum racket swing and coordination.
- *Failure to straighten the hitting arm* prevents contacting the ball with adequate momentum and at the highest possible point.
- *Shifting weight rearward* onto the right foot forces the body to lean back and reduces the reliability of the shot; furthermore, the body is not used in

hitting the ball.
- *Straightening the arm and bending the wrist too soon* before making contact interferes with acceleration in the movement (see fig. 90).
- *Premature planting of the right foot* in the direction of the shot destroys the overall coordination of the shot movement and makes hitting the ball at the highest possible point impossible (see fig. 91).
- *Thrusting the pelvis rearward* clearly indicates that the body was straightened too soon. As a result, the ball cannot be hit at the highest possible point (see fig. 92).
- *If the left arm swings past the body to the left,* this adds to body rotation even after contact and interferes with stability and control.

Follow-through
- *Accelerating the racket beyond the contact point* means that the ideal speed was not achieved at contact.

Fig. 88 Drawing the upper arm in toward the torso.

Fig. 89 Straightening the body too early.

Fig. 90 Straightening the elbow and using the wrist too early.

Fig. 91 Planting the right foot too early.

Fig. 92 Thrusting the pelvis rearward upon contact.

Straight Lob— Forehand and Backhand

In what situations and for what purposes is this technique used? What is the ball trajectory like?

Situations and Positions

- The straight lob is usually hit from the baseline area. However, sometimes it is hit from the area between the baseline and the service line.

Tactical Goals

- The ball should fly beyond the opponent, who is rushing or standing at the net. In other words, the ball should be hit to make it land as close as possible to the baseline, where the opponent cannot get to it or can make a return only with great difficulty. The lob is played especially when the opponent does not smash well, is close to the net, is running forward at high speed, or is facing the sun. The ball should be hit so that the opponent running to or standing near the net finds hitting a smash very difficult, assuming the ball is reachable at all. This is especially true if the ball falls steeply from a great height, when the opponent can reach it only behind the body or on the backhand side.

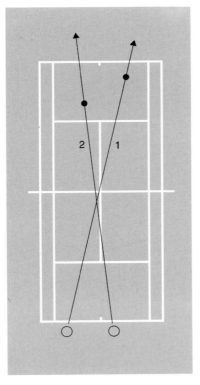

Fig. 93 Aiming points.

- Sometimes the straight lob—particularly at great height—is hit to break the opponent's rhythm or to break free from pressure applied by the opponent.
- It can also be used as a response to being lobbed over by the opponent after the player has attacked at the net or as a response to a lob by an opponent who has not moved forward from the baseline.

Effects on the Behavior of the Ball

- The ball should travel without much topspin or backspin.
- In playing over the opponent, the ball should fly neither too low, thereby avoiding a smash return, nor too high. Otherwise, the opponent will have enough time to run back to make the return.
- As a defensive move, the ball should be hit very high and fall as vertically as possible to create difficulties for the opponent.

Fig. 94 Flight of ball.

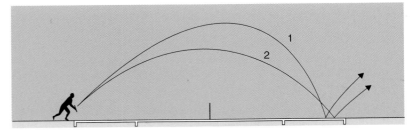

Fig. 95

What does the player do in a forehand and backhand lob to achieve the desired ball trajectory? What are these techniques used for?

Features of the Main Action Within the Stroke Phase

- The racket is swung with an open face in a forward and upward direction (illustrations 7–9).
- The racket is swung as far as possible in the direction of the shot (illustrations 7–9) to achieve great accuracy, distance, and safety.
- In comparison with the ground shot, the racket is swung with less acceleration to create greater accuracy and reliability.
- The ball is hit in front of the body and to one side with a wide open racket face (illustration 9) to achieve optimal energy transfer.

- Just before contact, the wrist assumes a position that corresponds to the desired departure speed to create the greatest degree of accuracy.
- Upon contact, the grip tightens and the wrist is held firmly for a brief instant to provide resistance to the ball.

Features of Supporting Actions

Backswing
- The racket is held with a forehand grip (or with a backhand grip for a straight backhand lob) so the ball can be hit far enough from the body.
- For a backhand lob, the left hand guides the racket back by its throat; this stabilizes the backswing and helps rotate the upper body to the rear.
- The upper body turns to the right (or to a slightly greater degree to the left with a straight backhand lob); the racket moves in a flat arc high

and to the rear to provide a fluid transition into the stroke movement (illustrations 3–6).
- The knees are bent fairly deeply (illustrations 5 and 6).

Stroke Phase
- In the transition to the stroke phase, the racket is brought significantly lower than the anticipated contact point. It is already open, especially for a straight backhand lob, thereby allowing the racket to be swung to the contact point in the stroke phase with the racket face in the right position.
- The left leg (or the right leg in a straight backhand lob), which is used as the support leg in the stroke and follow-through, has been moved forward in the anticipated shot direction (illustration 5). At this point, the feet should be greater than shoulder width apart to maintain balance.

- To support the upward movement in conjunction with the main action, the legs begin to straighten.
- The right arm remains slightly bent in a forehand lob and is straight in a backhand lob.
- The lateral foot position is maintained with both the forehand and the backhand lob. With a forehand lob, the upper body turns in the direction of the shot. With a backhand lob, the lateral position is maintained in order to meet the ball at the best point and to achieve good shot control.

Follow-through
- The racket swing ends relatively far in the direction of the shot and sharply forward and high (illustration 12).

- At the end of the follow-through phase, the racket is high above the head (illustration 12).

Possible Variations and Their Advantages and Disadvantages

Backswing
- Many players use the *semicontinental grip* even with the straight forehand and backhand lob. This presents no disadvantage, since with a straight lob, the acceleration of the movement and energy transfer in the main action are not so crucial and the racket face has to remain open at contact.
- The *upper part of the arc in the backswing* and the *timing and dynamics* of the movement can vary significantly among individuals, especially in the transition between taking the racket back in the backswing and moving it upward in the stroke phase.
- In a competitive situation, if a player wants to deceive the opponent about the intended shot and signal a ground shot, for example, then *the take back should approximate the backswing for a ground shot.*

Stroke Phase
- In many situations, the stroke is accomplished by *leaning back* with the upper body. This can be an advantage with fast oncoming balls and fairly high contact points since it helps in raising the racket high enough.

Follow-through
- The slower the stroke, the *shorter* the follow-through.

Common Flaws and Mistakes

Backswing

- *Little or no upper body rotation* interferes with the length of the backswing. In addition, in the stroke phase of a backhand lob, it prevents a smooth swing.
- *Failure to bend the knees* means no support is provided for the sharp upward movement of the racket in the main action. This also detracts from the timing and dynamics of the entire movement and the coordination of all the individual movements.

Stroke Phase

- *Failure to lower the racket head* reduces the sharp upward movement of the racket to the contact point (see fig. 96).
- *Straightening the legs too soon* especially interferes with the coordination of the swing in an upward and forward direction (see fig. 97).
- *Hitting the ball too late or too close to or too far away from the body* likewise detracts from shot control.

Follow-through

- *Ending the follow-through too early* by checking the movement of the racket has a very detrimental effect on ball control.

Fig. 96 Failure to lower the racket head.

- *Checking the movement* right after contact indicates that the swing and the ball control were defective.

Fig. 97 Straightening the legs too soon.

Smash

In what situations and for what purposes is this technique used? What is the ball trajectory like?

Situations and Positions

- Usually the smash is hit in midcourt (between the net and about 3 feet [1 m] behind the service line; see fig. 99, numbers 2 and 3).
- With a very long, high lob, a smash can be hit after the ball bounces in the vicinity of the baseline (see fig. 99, number 1).

Tactical Goals

- A good, reachable lob should be smashed in such a way (that is, hard and well placed) that the opponent cannot get to it.

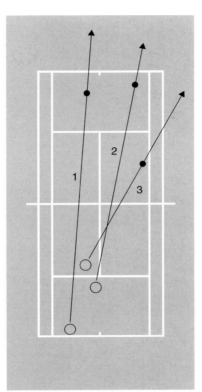

- A lob that is hard to reach should be smashed long and safe or a bit softer and at an angle. This gains some time for a good starting position for an attack.

Effects on Behavior of the Ball

- The ball can travel at very high speed and with very little spin.
- Instead, it can travel more slowly and with a little more spin.

Fig. 98 Aiming points.

Fig. 99 Ball flight.

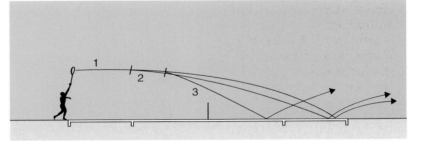

Fig. 100

What does the player do in a smash to achieve the desired ball trajectory? What is this technique used for?

Features of the Main Action Within the Stroke Phase

- The racket head accelerates steeply upward behind the back to give it the greatest speed at the contact point (illustrations 6–9).
- The ball is hit slightly in front of the head (illustration 9); at contact, the racket face tilts slightly forward to send the ball in the desired direction.
- By pronating the arm just before contacting the ball, the racket face is turned at a right angle to the flight direction (illustrations 8 and 9).

Features of Supporting Actions

Backswing
- The racket is held with a backhand grip to achieve the best possible contact point.
- In contrast with the serve, at the start of the backswing, the racket is brought to the upper right side of the body, mainly to save time (illustrations 1 and 2).
- Weight shifts to the right foot, which is to the rear (illustrations 1–4).
- The upper body leans back as it slightly turns on its axis to a lateral position relative to the trajectory of the lob (illustrations 1–4).
- To help maintain balance, the left arm stretches upward; this also helps in tipping the axis of the shoulders to the rear (illustrations 2 and 3).

Stroke Phase
- During the stroke, the upper body turns in the direction of the shot; the right shoulder moves higher than the left and supports the shot.
- The body stretches toward the contact point (see "Serve") in order to hit the ball at the highest point. Body and arm are fully stretched at the contact point (illustration 9), and the body weight is on the left foot.
- The racket is swung to the contact point at high speed through the lowest point of the loop.

Follow-through
- After making contact, the forearm rotates less than with the serve (illustrations 10 and 11), and the follow-through ends roughly in front of the left half

of the body. The wrist does not bend much to the right.

- The upper body follows the ball and continues to bend forward.
- The left arm moves in front of the body to help maintain balance.

Possible Variations and Their Advantages and Disadvantages

Backswing
- Many players hold the racket using the semicontinental grip.
- Many players take the racket back with a pendulum-like movement, as with the serve. Enough time may not be available to do this, especially with fast lobs, and doing so may retard the swing. In that case, a shorter pendulum motion is the goal. With many players, this pendulum action can produce a more harmonious overall movement.
- Depending on how far the lob is played over the left shoulder, *upper-body rotation and backward lean can vary greatly among individuals.*
- Many players assume a very open stroke position, especially when they have to move up for a smash.

Stroke Phase
- Many players extend the loop behind their back as far as with a serve; this can result in of hitting the ball less accurately.

Follow-through
- Sometimes the racket is swung *past the body to the left side* as with a serve.
- Hitting *using only the arm,* without involving the body,

Fig. 101 Bent racket arm.

may be necessary. Then the upper body would remain behind the contact point.

Common Flaws and Mistakes

Backswing
- Using a *forehand grip* makes hitting the ball at the highest point impossible.
- *Failure to rotate* the upper body means the acceleration path is not set up properly.
- *Failure to move up* in order to get under the ball for a short lob means the contact point is too far forward and too low, and the ball may be hit into the net.
- *Failure to bend the knees* makes transferring movement from low to high impossible.
- *Straightening the body too early* means that the ball will not be hit at the best contact point.

Fig. 102 Hitting the ball above the shoulder and to the side.

Stroke Phase
- *Failure to straighten the racket arm* causes the ball to be hit with a restricted swing motion and not at the highest possible point (see fig. 101).
- If *the racket follows the direction of the shot at an angle,* this gives the ball lots of spin and too little speed.
- *Hitting the ball above the right shoulder and to the side* means the ball is not hit at the best possible point (see fig. 102).

Follow-through
- A *very short follow-through* that ends shortly after making contact can indicate too little force was used or that the stroke movement was checked even before hitting the ball.

VARIATIONS IN TECHNIQUE

Topspin

In what situations and for what purposes is this technique used? What is the trajectory of the ball like?

Situations and Positions

- Forehand and backhand topspin are usually hit from near the baseline and from midcourt.

Tactical Goals

- The ball should hit the court about 6 to 10 feet (2 to 3 m) from the baseline so that the opponent is forced to stay behind the baseline to make returns (1).
- Topspin is used when safety is called for since even at high racket speeds, the ball is likely to land in bounds because of its trajectory.
- A long topspin shot often puts exceptional pressure onto an opponent. Since the ball bounces relatively high and fast, the opponent is forced far behind the baseline. If the opponent stays at the baseline, the ball has to be hit on the upward bounce or as a half volley, and that requires lots of experience to execute successfully.

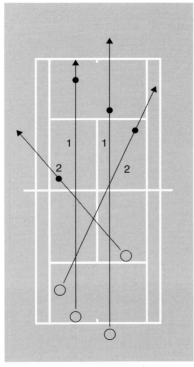

Fig. 103   Aiming points.

Fig. 104   Trajectory.

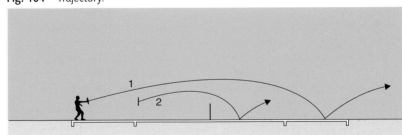

- The ball can be hit from mid-court in such a way that is goes across the court at an extreme angle and forces the opponent out-of-bounds (2).
- In a net attack by the opponent, this technique can also be used as a passing shot; this applies especially for a cross passing shot as well as for shots down the line. Topspin balls played straight at the opponent and low are very difficult to return since they have to be hit at lower-than-net height.

Effects on the Behavior of the Ball

- The ball may be hit with heavy topspin and into a high arcing trajectory.

Fig. 105

Topspin—Forehand

What does the player do in a forehand topspin shot to achieve the desired ball trajectory? What is this technique used for?

Features of the Main Action Within the Stroke Phase

- To achieve the desired heavy topspin, the racket head is swung forward and steeply upward against the ball (illustrations 5–8).
- The racket head must be traveling at a very high rate of speed to give the ball the desired topspin.
- The ball is hit at the side and in front of the body using a vertical racket face (illustration 8) to achieve optimal energy transfer.
- Just before contact, the wrist is brought into a position that corresponds to the departure velocity to achieve the greatest degree of accuracy.

- At contact, the grip tightens and the wrist is held firmly for a brief instant to provide resistance to the ball.

Features of Supporting Actions

Backswing
- The racket is held with the extreme forehand grip so that at contact, the racket face is vertical and an efficient transfer of energy occurs.
- The right leg, which is used as the support leg (anchor leg) in the stroke movement, is fully weighted in a long side step (illustrations 1–3), and both knees are deeply bent (illustration 3).
- The upper body is turned to the rear to create tension in the muscles. The left arm supports the turn.
- The racket is brought back (illustrations 1–3) to afford a smooth transition into the stroke phase.

Stroke Phase
- The racket head is lowered beneath the anticipated contact point (illustrations 5 and 6); this allows the player to swing the end of the racket sharply upward at contact.
- An explosive straightening of the legs begins with the smooth transition between the backswing and the stroke. It starts from a more or less open stroke position where the right leg—the one that corresponds to the racket arm—pushes off forcefully from the court surface (illustrations 5–7).
- The upper body turns toward the front simultaneously with the stroke movement in a frontal position (illustrations 5–8); this allows the racket to be swung steeply upward and forward for the best energy transfer.

Follow-through
- The pronounced forward and upward movement of the racket head continues (illustration 9); this ends the shot and shows that the ball has been given the desired spin.

- Finally, the racket swings to the left side of the body. This is followed by a weight shift to the left leg. Both actions—arm movement and weight transfer—are accomplished through movements in the stroke phase, that is, by bracing with the right leg and simultaneously turning the upper body.

Possible Variations and Their Advantages and Disadvantages

Backswing
- *The use of the forehand grip can vary a lot* among individuals; topspin players typically tend to use the extreme forehand grip.
- Often the follow-through is accomplished by lifting the elbow high and to the rear (see photo) so that the racket face points downward. Also, the position can vary; the more the extreme forehand grip is used, the more open the position. The more the body is used, the more the ball should be hit cross court

and the more the shot is intended to set up a net attack.

- The *timing and dynamics* also vary a lot among individuals, especially in the transition between taking the racket back in the backswing phase and accelerating it in the stroke phase.

Stroke Phase

- Many players *straighten the support leg* (anchor leg) with such explosiveness that both feet are off the ground just before or after the shot.
- Simultaneous rotation of the body twists the player partly around so that the right leg is to the front and the left is to the rear.
- The stroke movement continues by means of significant *upper-body rotation.*
- To increase the speed of the hit, the *arm* can be more or less *bent* during the stroke.

Follow-through

- When the forearm is used forcefully in combination with a high contact point in the stroke phase, *the racket is tipped quickly and sharply* toward the left hip (as in a windshield wiper motion).

- The racket can be swung over the right shoulder. This topspin is usually employed with a low contact point.

After hitting a topspin shot from a high contact point, the racket swings toward the left hip.

Fig. 106   Too little upper-body rotation.

Fig. 107   Exaggerated lateral stroke position.

Fig. 108   Hitting from the shoulder.

Common Flaws and Mistakes

Backswing

- Using the *semicontinental or backhand grip* makes efficient energy transfer impossible.
- *Little or no upper body rotation* (fig. 106) greatly restricts the backswing.
- An *insufficient bend in the knees* (fig. 107) makes weighting and bending the right leg more difficult and interferes with upper-body rotation in the stroke phase.

Stroke Phase

- *Failure to lower the racket head* beneath the anticipated contact point makes swinging the racket in a pronounced forward and upward direction impossible.
- *Straightening the legs too early* destroys the coordination of the entire movement.
- *Leaning back* makes controlling the position of the racket head at contact harder. The forward movement of the racket decreases, and the ball flies too high and too short.
- *Inadequate racket acceleration,* especially at the end of the racket, gives the ball too little topspin and velocity.

- *Hitting the ball using a movement from only the shoulder* and with a straight arm (fig. 108) is an inefficient way to accelerate the racket.
- *Hitting the ball too far from or too close to the body* fails to make efficient use of the body.

Follow-through

- A *very short follow-through* is a sign that the swing was checked before contact or was inadequate from its start.

Fig. 109

Topspin—Backhand

> What does the player do in a backhand topspin shot to achieve the desired ball trajectory? What is this technique used for?

Features of the Main Action Within the Stroke Phase

- The racket—especially the racket head—is swung forward and steeply upward against the ball to give it the desired heavy topspin (illustration 8).
- The racket must travel at a high rate of speed to transmit the desired topspin to the ball.
- The ball is hit to the side and farther from the body than with a forehand topspin shot. The racket face is at a right angle to the shot (illustration 9) in the interest of efficient energy transfer.

- Just before contact, the wrist is placed into a position that corresponds to the departure velocity to create the greatest degree of accuracy.
- At contact, the grip tightens, and the wrist is held firmly for a brief instant to provide resistance to the oncoming ball.

Features of Supporting Actions

Backswing

- The racket is held with the backhand grip to provide a vertical racket face at contact and an efficient transfer of energy.
- At the start of the backswing, the left hand guides the racket back by its throat (illustrations 1 and 2) to provide a smooth transition to the stroke movement.
- The upper body turns sharply to the rear so that the right

half of the back points to the net (illustration 5). The tensing of the muscles of the torso supports the acceleration of the arm in the direction of the shot.
- The right leg, which is placed to the front, accepts the weight transfer. The feet are kept more than hip width apart to improve balance.
- The knees are sharply bent.

Stroke Phase

- The racket is brought below the anticipated contact point (illustrations 5–8) so the racket head can be swung steeply upward in the stroke phase (illustrations 8 and 9).
- The legs, particularly the forward anchor leg, are used to support the steep upward movement (illustrations 6–9).

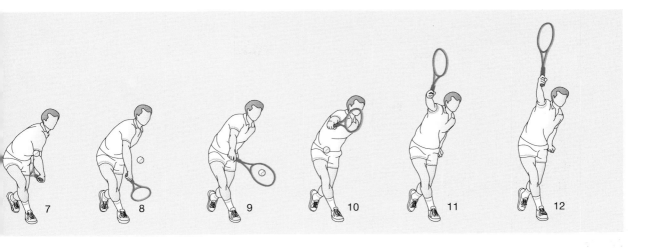

- The upper body turns.
- The ball is hit using a straight arm (illustration 9); often the arm straightens just before making contact.

Follow-through
- The steep upward movement of the racket continues in the direction of the shot, and the lateral position is maintained (illustrations 10 and 11).
- At the end of the follow-through, the body turns as a result of the forceful and rapid forward swing, thereby producing an open position.

Possible Variations and Their Advantages and Disadvantages

Backswing
- The *backhand grip* can vary significantly among individuals; many representative topspin players tend to use an extreme backhand grip.
- The *timing and dynamics* can also vary among individuals, particularly in the transition between taking the racket back in the backswing phase and accelerating it in the stroke phase.

Stroke Phase
- Many players *straighten the support leg* so explosively that both feet are in the air just after contact.
- When the forearm is used strongly in the stroke phase in conjunction with the extreme backhand grip, the *arm* is *bent* to a greater or lesser degree to increase racket speed and to

intensify the steep upward movement at contact. These variations, however, require considerable strength in the forearm.

Follow-through
- When the body is heavily involved in the main action, this can lead to an open position and a follow-through where the racket points *in a direction opposite the shot.*
- When the forearm is used strongly in the stroke phase, the *racket may tip to the right* (like the action of a windshield wiper) accompanied by the upper body leaning more or less backward.
- With an extreme backhand grip and an accompanying very early contact point, *the upward movement of the arm continues* in the follow-through phase. The angle between the forearm and the racket remains practically constant.

Common Flaws and Mistakes

Backswing
- Using the *semicontinental or forehand grip* does not provide optimal energy transfer.
- *Little or no upper-body rotation and inadequate backswing* make accelerating the racket sufficiently impossible to accomplish.
- *Failure to assume a lateral position* shortens the backswing.

Stroke Phase
- *Failure to lower the racket head* under the anticipated contact point (fig. 110) makes swinging the racket forward and steeply upward impossible.
- *Straightening the legs too soon* interferes with coordinating the movements that make up the stroke.

Fig. 110   Failure to lower the racket head and premature straightening of the right leg.

- If *the lateral position is not held long enough,* the entire body rotates with the stroke movement. As a result, hitting the ball accurately is harder.
- *Inadequate racket acceleration,* especially of the end of the racket, does not give the ball enough topspin or speed.
- *Hitting the ball too late or too far away from the body* also interferes with adequate racket acceleration and efficient energy transfer.

Follow-through
- A *very short upward movement* due to checking the flow of the movement indicates that the racket swing was checked before making contact or was inadequate at its beginning.

The racket arm straightens
before making contact.

Two-handed Topspin—Backhand

The two-handed backhand top-spin shot is used in the same situations and with the same purposes as the one-handed shot. Pages 90–91 detailed the main criteria of the two-handed shot.

Here are the most important features:

- The racket is held with both hands in a forehand grip (often in an extreme forehand grip).
- In comparison with the one-handed shot, the racket head is often brought lower in the transition between backswing and stroke phase. This makes swinging the end of the racket faster and more steeply upward to achieve the desired topspin in the stroke phase impossible. In practice, players who use a two-handed backhand achieve greater topspin than comparable players who hit with one hand.
- The shot is often hit from an open position.
- With a one-handed backhand topspin shot, the upper body remains in a lateral position for a longer time. However, when using two hands, it is already turned in the direction of the shot in the stroke phase because of the way the hands grasp the racket.

In the stroke phase, the upper body turns in the direction of the shot.

Slice

In what situations and for what purposes is this technique used? What is the ball trajectory like?

Situations and Positions

- The forehand and backhand slice are usually hit from the area near the baseline and from the area between the service line and the baseline. The slice is hit much more frequently with the backhand than with the forehand.

Tactical Goals

- The ball must remain in play.
- The ball should be played in such a way that it bounces as close as possible to the opponent's baseline. This forces the opponent to stay behind the baseline.
- A slice played short should bounce low and force the opponent into an awkward, low contact point.
- A serve by the opponent is often returned as a slice. This may occur on a first serve for reasons of time and safety or on the second serve when the ball from the attacking player is to be played in front of the feet.
- A slice helps change the tempo of the rally and break the opponent's rhythm. Balls nearly out of reach or that can be hit only under duress can be hit fairly safely and accurately with a slice.

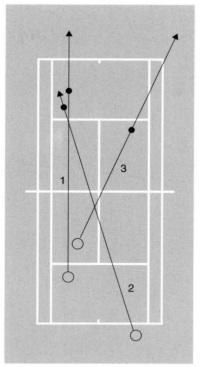

Fig. 111   Aiming points.

- Shots from the opponent that end up too short are a welcome opportunity to attack. This attack shot is often played as a slice because:
  - the ball can be hit comfortably as it rises;
  - accuracy is good due to the relatively slow stroke;
  - the controlled stroke and the body movements blend together well and provide a smooth transition into a run forward;
  - The relatively slow ball flight makes getting into a good position at the net possible.
- A high-bouncing ball is returned as a slice on the up-bounce to keep the player from being driven back too far.

Effects on Behavior of the Ball

- The ball should have a lot of backspin.
- The ball should travel at a medium speed.

Fig. 112   Ball trajectory.

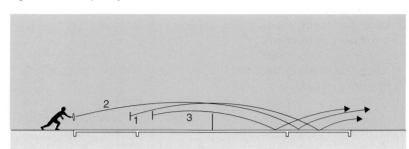

Fig. 113

Slice—Forehand

What does the player do in a forehand slice to achieve the desired ball trajectory? What is this technique used for?

Features of the Main Action Within the Stroke Phase

- The racket moves in a shallow arc from above and behind to below and in front (illustrations 6–8) to create backspin.
- The racket is accelerated slightly up to the contact point to create the necessary racket speed for the desired spin.
- The racket swings as far as possible in the direction of the shot in the interest of safety and accuracy.
- The ball is hit in front of the body with a nearly vertical

racket face (fig. 8) to afford an efficient transfer of energy.
- Just before contact, the wrist is placed into a position that corresponds with the departure velocity to create the greatest degree of accuracy.
- At contact, the grip is tightened, and the wrist is held firmly for a brief instant to provide resistance to the ball.

Features of Supporting Actions

Backswing

- For a forehand slice, the racket is held with the forehand grip.
- The upper body and the right leg are turned to the right side; the racket is brought upward and to the rear above the anticipated contact point (illustrations 1 and 2).
- The racket arm is slightly bent, the upper arm is fairly far from

the upper body, the racket face is nearly vertical, and the racket head is higher than the player's head (illustration 2).
- At the end of the backswing phase, the left leg advances in the anticipated direction of the shot (illustration 3); the feet are kept greater than hip width apart to maintain balance.

Stroke Phase

- The transition from the backswing to the stroke movement directed forward and down follows a shallow arc in a fluid movement (illustrations 3–5).
- The weight transfer is forward and down onto the front leg. Both knees bend (illustrations 3–8) and support the stroke movement.
- The upper body turns in the direction of the shot (illustrations 6–8); this supports the stroke movement and helps create an ideal contact point.

Follow-through

- The follow-through continues forward and down (illustration 9); this indicates that the shot was made correctly.
- The follow-through ends forward and high, and the racket face continues to open up. At the end of the follow-through, the racket is even with or above the player's head (illustrations 11 and 12).

Possible Variations and Their Advantages and Disadvantages

Backswing

- Many players use the *semicontinental grip* for the forehand slice; this has an advantage at low contact points since the racket face needs to be slightly open in such cases. At high contact points, this grip is a disadvantage since presenting a vertical racket face to the ball is very difficult.

- The *height and length of the backswing* can vary significantly among individuals. A shorter and flatter backswing for fast oncoming balls makes starting the stroke in a timely manner possible. A very long and high backswing, on the other hand, contributes to a fast swing but may reduce ball control.
- The *shallow arc* in the transition from backswing to stroke *may be done away with*. In certain situations, this may contribute to greater shot control, but it may detract from rhythm, flow of motion, and racket acceleration.
- The *timing and dynamics* of the movement may also vary greatly among individuals, especially in the transition between taking the racket back in the backswing phase and accelerating it in the stroke phase. Taking the racket back early and pausing at the end of

the backswing allows for a controlled stroke movement. If the racket is taken back later, the transition to the stroke movement is more fluid but potentially less controlled.

Stroke Phase

- For reasons of time, with fast oncoming balls (for example, the first service), a *considerably shortened stroke* directed forward and sharply upward is used.

Follow-through

- The more controlled and longer the stroke, the *longer* the follow-through.
- With short strokes, the follow-through can be so *short* forward and upward that it is scarcely visible.
- In certain situations (for example, returning a slow serve or a short cross passing shot), the follow-through forward and upward can be shortened.

Common Flaws and Mistakes

Backswing

- When using the *backhand grip,* at the ideal contact point, the racket face is not vertical.
- *Little or no upper body rotation* leads to a punching movement by straightening the arm, or the racket swings past the body to the left side, producing sidespin.
- With *late follow-through,* the desired controlled stroke is not possible, and the ball is often not hit at the best-possible instant.
- If using *improper form in follow-through* and the upper arm is held too close to the body, a punching motion results.
- If *at the end of the backswing the racket head is not raised above the anticipated contact point,* the stroke cannot be made from high to low.

Stroke Phase

- *Failure to bend the knee of the forward leg* (fig. 114) creates no weight transfer forward and downward to support the stroke.

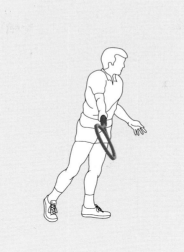

Fig. 114   Failure to bend knee of forward leg.

Fig. 115   Very open racket face at contact.

- *Failure to maintain lateral position and turning in the hips and upper body too early* means the stroke takes place to the left in front of the body, and accuracy in hitting the ball suffers.
- *Hitting the ball with an excessively open racket face* (fig. 115) causes the ball to pick up too little speed and fly too high.
- *Hitting the ball too late or too near or too far from the body* means the ball is given too little speed and spin, and control is greatly reduced.

Follow-through

- *Stopping the follow-through too early* by checking the flow of the movement indicates that the stroke was checked too soon and that ball control was deficient.
- *Bending the arm too soon and too much,* accompanied by a movement of the racket hand toward the left shoulder, indicates impaired ball control.

The upper body has been turned in the direction of the shot, and the contact point is in front of the body.

Fig. 116

Slice—Backhand

What does the player do in a backhand slice to achieve the desired ball trajectory? What is this technique used for?

Features of the Main Action Within the Stroke Phase

- The movement of the racket is in a shallow arc from low to high and from rear to front to produce backspin.
- The racket is accelerated slightly up to the contact point to create the necessary speed for the desired spin.
- The racket is swung as far as possible in the direction of the shot in the interest of safety and accuracy.
- The ball is hit at the side and in front of the body (illustration 10) for the best-possible energy transfer.

- Just before contact, the wrist is brought into a position that corresponds with the departure speed to create the greatest degree of accuracy.
- At contact, the grip is tightened, and the wrist is held firmly for a brief instant to provide resistance to the ball.

Features of Supporting Actions

Backswing

- For a backhand slice, the racket is held with a backhand grip.
- The upper body and the left leg are turned to the left; the upper body rotation is much more pronounced than with a forehand slice. The racket is taken back to a height above the anticipated contact point (illustration 2).
- During the backswing, the left hand remains at the throat of the racket (illustrations 1–6) to stabilize the backswing and help in turning the upper body.

- At the end of the backswing, the arm is bent. The upper arm is a good distance away from the body. The racket face is very open. The racket head is at shoulder height (illustration 6).
- During the backswing, the right leg is advanced in the anticipated direction of the shot; the feet are kept greater than hip width apart to maintain balance.

Stroke Phase

- The transition from the backswing to the downward and forward stroke movement follows a shallow arc in order to create a fluid movement. In contrast with the forehand slice, the loop is a bit smaller.
- Weight is transferred forward and downward onto the leading leg; the knees bend in support of the stroke (illustrations 7–10).
- During the stroke, the arm is straightened to achieve an ideal contact point. At the same time,

the forearm turns (supination) so that the racket face is nearly vertical at contact and energy transfers efficiently (illustrations 7–10).

- The lateral position of the feet and body is maintained up to and through the contact point (illustrations 7–12) for the best possible ball control.

Follow-through

- In the follow-through, the racket is swung forward and downward (illustrations 11 and 12); this indicates that the stroke was done properly.
- The follow-through ends forward and upward with the racket face open; at the end of the movement, the racket hand is at shoulder height.

Possible Variations and Their Advantages and Disadvantages

Backswing

- Many players use the *semicontinental grip* for the backhand slice. This is advantageous with low contact points where the racket face needs to be slightly open. This grip is a disadvantage with high contact points because presenting a vertical racket face at contact is difficult. Generally speaking, the semi-continental grip makes transferring energy efficiently in a backhand slice difficult to accomplish.
- *The height and length* of the backswing can vary a lot among individuals. Reduced body rotation and taking the elbow back a shorter distance, usually in conjunction with a lower backswing, make hitting fast oncoming balls at the right contact point possible. Those factors reduce the smoothness and momentum of the movement, however. The stroke

then comes principally from the forearm. A long and high backswing, combined with pronounced upper-body rotation and a long take back in the elbow, where the right hand comes close to the left shoulder, makes hitting the ball with lots of momentum and high speed possible. On the other hand, this may interfere with control. With a backswing that lifts the elbow high, the racket head often points downward and accelerates in an upward direction by turning the arm at the start of the stroke phase.

- *Many players keep the arm straight during the backswing.* Control is good, but the speed of the hit is reduced.
- The *timing and dynamics* of the movement also vary among individuals, especially in the transition between taking the racket back and accelerating it in the stroke phase. An early backswing with a hesitation at the end of the take back permits a controlled

stroke. With a later backswing, the transition from take back to stroke is more fluid, but it is often less controlled.

Stroke Phase

- For reasons of time, a *greatly shortened stroke* is used with fast oncoming balls; it is directed mainly forward and steeply upward.
- The stroke moves slightly *left to right,* imparting sidespin to the ball.
- Players often differ in the extent to which they *straighten their arm* in the stroke. Straightening the arm just before making contact increases the speed of the shot and encourages hitting the ball early. However, that makes controlling the ball harder. Straightening the arm earlier (as in the photos on pages 134 and 135) improves control but reduces the speed of the shot.

Follow-through

- *The more controlled and the longer the stroke,* the longer the follow-through.
- With short strokes, the follow-through forward and upward can be so *short* that it is scarcely noticeable.
- In certain situations (for example, returning a slow serve or a short cross passing shot), the follow-through forward and upward may likewise be shortened.
- With a slice involving *additional sidespin,* the follow-through is often shorter and directed upward and to the right.

Common Flaws and Mistakes

Backswing

- Using the *forehand grip* means the racket face is not vertical at the ideal contact point.
- *Little or no upper-body rotation* results in the stroke not following the direction of the shot but, rather, too far to the right in front of the body (thereby producing sidespin).
- With *late backswing,* the required control in the stroke is no longer possible, and often the ball is not hit at the right instant.

Stroke Phase

- *Failure to bend the forward knee* creates no weight transfer forward and downward in support of the stroke.
- *Failure to maintain lateral position long enough* rotates the body to the right with the shot, the ball picks up lots of sidespin, and ball control is less than desirable.
- A *very open racket face at contact* means the ball picks up too little speed and flies too high.
- *Failure to straighten the arm* during the stroke (fig. 117) causes the momentum of the stroke and control to not be what they should.

Fig. 117   Failure to straighten the arm.

Fig. 118   Follow-through low and to the right.

- *Hitting the ball too late, too close to, or too far from the body* gives the ball too little speed and spin and greatly undermines control.

Follow-through

- *Deviating very early* from the direction of the shot is evidence that the ball has picked up more sidespin than backspin.

- *Failure to end the follow-through* forward and upward means the movement is checked strongly. To bring the shot under control, the wrist is often bent forward so that the back of the hand points in the direction of the shot, and the racket often tips further down and to the right (as in fig. 118).

Drop Shot

In what situations and for
what purposes is this technique used? What is the
ball trajectory like?

Situations and Positions
- The forehand and backhand
  drop shot are usually hit from
  the area between the service
  line and the baseline.

Tactical Goals
- The purpose of a drop shot is to
  draw a baseline player up to
  the net.
- A drop shot forces the opponent to run, and this tactic can
  be used to tire the opponent.
- A drop shot makes scoring a
  direct point possible if the
  opponent is far away or moving
  in a direction opposite that of
  the drop ball.
- The ball should be played in
  such a way that it lands just
  behind the net.

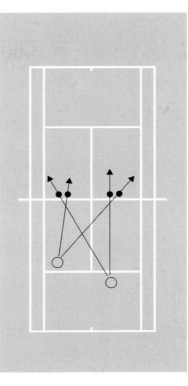

- The ball should not bounce
  very high or far in order to keep
  the opponent from getting to
  it. At least, this should force a
  very low contact point just
  before the second bounce.
- If the opponent plays a drop
  shot, the player can score a
  direct point with a counterdrop
  or at least get into a good position on the court.

Effects on the Behavior of the Ball
- The ball may have strong backspin.
- The ball may fly in such a way
  that it drops steeply right behind
  the net.

Fig. 119 Aiming points (*left*).

Fig. 120 Ball trajectory (*below*).

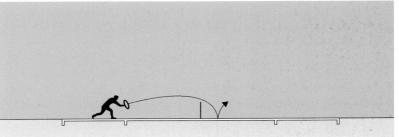

Fig. 121

Drop Shot—Forehand and Backhand

What does the player do in a forehand or backhand drop shot to achieve the desired ball trajectory? What is this technique used for?

Features of the Main Action Within the Stroke Phase

- The racket moves from high and behind to forward and low (illustrations 4–7) to produce backspin.
- The racket is swung relatively slowly to the contact point. On the one hand, this stops a fast ball effectively. On the other, it avoids giving too much speed to a slow ball.
- The contact point is in front of the body and to the side. The racket face is nearly vertical (illustration 7) but increasingly open at lower contact points to produce the desired flight curve.

- Just before contact, the wrist is brought into a position that corresponds to the departure velocity to create the greatest degree of accuracy.

Features of Supporting Actions

Backswing

- For a forehand drop shot, the racket is held with a forehand grip; a backhand grip is used for a backhand drop shot.
- The backswing is relatively short to avoid creating too much momentum at the contact point.
- At the start of the backswing, the upper body is turned to the rear (illustrations 1–3); the left hand remains at the throat of the racket in the backswing for a backhand drop shot.
- The head of the racket is brought considerably higher than the anticipated contact point; the racket face is vertical or slightly closed (illustration 3).

- The left leg is placed to the side for a forehand drop shot. With a backhand drop shot, the right leg is moved to the side (illustrations 3 and 4). The feet are kept greater than hip width apart to maintain balance.

Stroke Phase

- During the stroke, the leg closer to the net is bent at the knee (illustrations 4–7) in support of the movement directed forward and backward; this also contributes to coordination between arm movement and weight shift.
- For a forehand drop shot, the upper body is turned slightly in the direction of the shot (illustrations 6 and 7). For a backhand drop shot, the lateral position is maintained to create an ideal contact point and good ball control.
- The racket arm is nearly straight at the contact point in a backhand drop shot. With a forehand drop shot, the racket arm is slightly bent (illustration 7).

Follow-through

- Just after the ball is hit is a short follow-through forward and down (illustrations 8–9). This indicates that the speed of the shot and the spin were appropriately adjusted to meet the purpose of the drop shot. Subsequently, a short movement forward and upward occurs (illustration 10).
- The forearm is turned (supination with a forehand and pronation with a backhand shot), and the racket face is directed nearly parallel to the ground (illustration 10). This keeps the follow-through appropriately short.
- The leg closer to the net is straightened, thereby supporting the upward movement of the follow-through and helping to coordinate arm and body movements (illustration 10).

Possible Variations and Their Advantages and Disadvantages

Backswing

- Many players use the *semicontinental grip* for a forehand and backhand drop shot; this facilitates the desired open racket face following contact.
- A *fairly long backswing*—as with a slice shot—avoids signaling an intended drop shot to the opponent.
- The *racket face* may be *quite closed* at the end of the backswing, especially with a forehand drop shot. This makes getting the racket face into the right position at contact easier, and the follow-through can be appropriately short and smooth.

Stroke Phase

- With relatively fast oncoming balls, *the forward movement is usually minimal.* The ball is nearly stopped and is given strong backspin.
- At contact, the racket face can be more or less open. It is often open for a low contact point and when the ball is hit as it drops in an arc after bouncing; that way the ball can be hit safely over the net. The racket face opens up in proportion to the anticipated height of the shot trajectory.

Follow-through

- The *height and length of the follow-through* vary according to the scope of the stroke.
- For a drop shot on a fast oncoming ball, *the follow-through is not directed upward* but, rather, forward and down in the direction of the shot. The racket face is not opened further, the stroke is checked suddenly, the movement has no flow or smooth ending, and the racket face is in a good position at the contact point.

Common Faults and Mistakes

Backswing

- *Failure to turn the upper body* means a basic requirement is missing for a controlled and satisfying shot.
- *Failure to raise the racket head above the anticipated contact point* makes impossible a stroke directed forward and downward. Therefore, controlling the height and length of the ball is harder.
- *Late follow-through* means the required control is missing from the stroke, and ball control suffers greatly.

Stroke Phase

- *Turning the forearm (pronation in a backhand drop shot and supination in a forehand drop shot) and opening up the racket face before making contact with the ball* (fig. 122) means the ball picks up the desired backspin but flies too high. Control over the length of the ball flight is usually lacking.

Fig. 122   Opening up the racket face too much before contacting the ball.

- *A stroke that carries too much momentum* makes controlling the departure velocity and the length of the shot practically impossible.
- *Failure to bend the leg nearer the net* detracts from coordination of the movement in the entire body. The stroke is produced with only the arm, adversely affecting shot control.
- *Straightening the forward leg too early* often produces a weight shift upward and rearward. It destroys coordination of the movement, and the ball flight is too short and high.
- Having a *relaxed wrist at contact* means the oncoming ball is stopped effectively, but control is lacking over spin and trajectory.

Follow-through

- *Following through too fast and too far* is a sign that the racket was moving too fast at contact and that the oncoming ball was not stopped adequately. The player had no control over spin and length of trajectory.

Drop Volley

In what situations and for what purposes is this technique used? What is the ball trajectory like?

Situations and Positions

- The drop volley is played close to the net, especially when the contact is at or below the level of the net.

Tactical Goals

- The ball should be played in such a way that it bounces right behind the net and the opponent cannot get to it.
- The cross drop volley should be played away from the opponent and at an acute angle to the net to score a direct point.

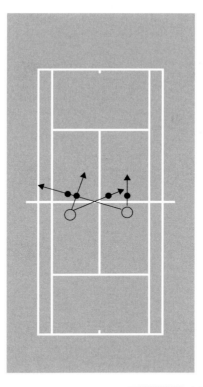

- A drop volley is often suited to low or topspin passing shots from the opponent since hitting a drop shot from a low contact point far into the court can be difficult.

Effects on Behavior of the Ball

- The ball should pick up backspin.
- The ball should be slow.
- The ball should not fly too high over the net.

Fig. 123   Aiming points (*left*).

Fig. 124   Ball trajectory (*below*).

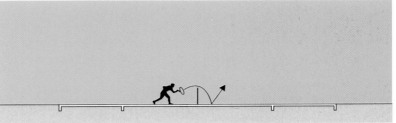

Fig. 125

Drop Volley— Forehand and Backhand

> What does the player do in a drop volley to achieve the desired ball trajectory? What is this technique used for?

Features of the Main Action Within the Stroke Phase

- A short follow-through in a forward and downward direction creates backspin.
- The racket moves at very low speed to stop the oncoming ball.
- The contact point is in front of the body (illustration 3); at contact, the racket face is more or less open.

Features of Supporting Actions

Backswing

- The drop volley is played on the forehand side using a forehand grip and on the backhand side with a backhand grip.
- The upper body is turned slightly to the rear. The backswing rearward and upward is very short since very little momentum is needed for the shot (illustrations 1 and 2).

Stroke Phase

- During the stroke movement directed forward and downward, the leg closer to the net is bent at the knee (illustrations 2 and 3) to set up an ideal contact point; the arm movement is carefully coordinated with the weight shift.
- At the contact point, the racket arm is practically straight (illustration 3). A good drop shot is made primarily through supination of the wrist in the forehand or pronation in the backhand.
- During the stroke, the upper body remains relatively quiet to increase precision of the hit.

Follow-through

- A short follow-through forward and upward occurs. Often, the racket is pushed rearward and downward by fast oncoming balls.

Possible Variations and Their Advantages and Disadvantages

Backswing

- The short *backswing can be eliminated.* In other words, the racket is brought forward directly toward the contact point. This results in an early contact point and a consequent reduction in momentum.

Stroke Phase

- Control over the length and height of a drop shot comes from the position of the racket face at the contact point. This involves *supination of the forearm in the forehand and pronation in the backhand.*
- Many players hit the ball with a *bent arm.* The contact point is thus closer to the body, and that may lead to better ball control.

- *The forward and downward movement of the racket may be eliminated.* The racket is simply held a the correct angle at the contact point, and the ball rebounds from the racket face. This type of drop volley shot requires lots of feel for the ball.
- *The racket face is held at an angle to the oncoming ball.* A firm wrist at contact causes the ball to bounce into the narrow angle formed with the net. The disadvantage of a fairly long drop shot is canceled by its flight in a direction away from the opponent.

Follow-through

- *The nature of the follow-through* depends on how far the racket is moved forward and downward to the make contact.
- The follow-through may be *eliminated* entirely.

Common Flaws and Mistakes

Backswing

- *A long backswing* deceives the opponent into expecting a normal volley. However, achieving the low racket speed in the main action is difficult since the stroke needs to be checked.

Stroke Phase

- A *very long and rapid stroke* transfers too much energy to the ball, which is hit too far.
- A *late and high contact point* adversely affects ball control.
- A *relaxed wrist* interferes with control.

Follow-through

- A *very pronounced and high follow-through* indicates that the stroke movement was too rapid and the shot was too high.

Half Volley

In what situations and for what purposes is this technique used? What is the ball trajectory like?

Situations and Positions
- The forehand and backhand half volleys are usually played near the service line. The half volleys is thus used when the player is standing too close to the point where the ball lands to hit it as a ground stroke yet too far away to hit it as a volley. The half volley can also be hit from other positions on the court.

Tactical Goals
- Playing a half volley keeps a player from being forced far out of the court. The player can avoid hitting the ball while moving backward.
- In situations where the direction and speed of a bouncing ball are difficult to predict because of topspin, sidespin, wind, and an uneven court surface, the ball can be returned with a degree of safety using a half volley.
- A half volley can speed up the game. It puts pressure onto the opponent since the ball returns to that side of the net so quickly.

Effects on the Behavior of the Ball
- The ball may be played at medium to high speed.
- The ball may cross the net as flat as possible.

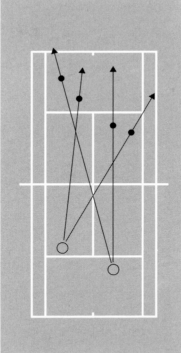

Fig. 126 Aiming points (*left*).

Fig. 127 Ball flight (*below*).

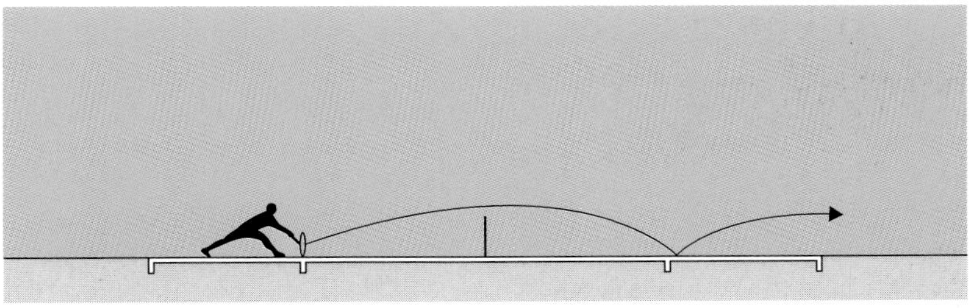

The ball is played as a half volley right after it bounces in the midcourt area.

Fig. 128

Half Volley— Forehand and Backhand

What does the player do in a half volley to achieve the desired ball trajectory? What is this technique used for?

Features of the Main Action Within the Stroke Phase

- The movement of the racket begins practically parallel to the court surface (figures 6–8) so the ball can be hit immediately after it bounces.
- The racket is accelerated up to the contact point.
- The ball is hit at a level even with the foot closer to the net (illustration 8) to afford an optimal energy transfer.
- The racket face is nearly vertical at the contact point.
- Just before contact, the wrist is brought into a position that corresponds to the departure velocity to create the greatest degree of accuracy.
- At contact, the grip is tightened and the wrist is held firmly for a brief instant to provide resistance to the ball.

Features of the Main Action

Backswing

- The racket is held with a forehand grip for a forehand half volley and with a backhand grip for a backhand half volley.
- The upper body turns to the rear to support the backswing (illustrations 1–3).
- The backswing follows a straight line to the rear; the racket makes a shallow loop and is swung forward nearly parallel to the court surface (illustrations 3–5).
- The knees bend sharply to aid in lowering the racket head to the level of the anticipated contact point (illustrations 5–7).

- The foot closer to the net is planted far ahead to help maintain balance in this low position (illustrations 5–8).

Stroke Phase

- The racket is swung flat and parallel to the court surface.
- The transition from the backswing to the stroke phase occurs without interruption to keep the movement fluid.
- During the stroke, the body weight is transferred decisively onto the leading leg, which remains deeply bent (illustrations 5–8).

Follow-through

- The follow-through is a movement forward and upward; the leading leg remains more or less bent (illustrations 9–12).

Possible Variations and Their Advantages and Disadvantages

Backswing

- The racket can also be held with a *semicontinental grip.* However, with a backhand half volley, this can make presenting the racket face in the right position difficult for an early contact point.
- The backswing can be *relatively long,* provided that adequate time is available and that the ball is to be played hard from the vicinity of the baseline, from midcourt, or near the net as a topspin shot.
- *The backswing can also be done rearward and downward* for a quicker alignment with the anticipated contact point.

Stroke Phase

- *According to the situation, the contact point can be between the midpoint of the body and the foot closer to the net* or in front of the leading foot.
- The *length of the stroke* varies in accordance with the location of the contact point; the stroke is long for a contact point far away from the body but short for a later contact point.
- *The position of the racket face* for a half volley varies according to position on the court. Close to the net it is more open, and it is more vertical near the baseline.
- In a topspin half volley, the stroke movement is directed strongly forward and upward.
- *The length of the step* with the forward foot and the accompanying weight transfer are adjusted according to the distance from the contact point.

Follow-through

- At high stroke speed, the *follow-through is forward and high in the direction of the shot.*
- With a half volley at net height and a topspin half volley, the *follow-through is sharply forward and upward* in accordance with the direction of the stroke.
- The follow-through is aided by straightening the forward leg somewhat.

Technique

Common Flaws and Mistakes

Backswing
- *Bending the rear leg too late or not at all* makes lining up with the low contact point impossible.
- A *very high backswing* makes getting the racket to the right contact point in time very difficult.

Stroke Phase
- With *insufficient bend in the knees,* the racket head must be pointed downward to hit the ball close to the court surface. This adversely affects weight shift and energy transfer.

Fig. 129 Straightening the forward leg too soon and pointing the racket head downward.

- When *straightening the forward leg too soon* (fig. 129), the leg is already straight before the ball is hit. In other words, the ball cannot be hit just above the court surface, and shot control is reduced.

Follow-through
- If the follow-through is completely suppressed, shot control suffers greatly.

Slice Lob and Topspin Lob— Forehand and Backhand

In what situations and for what purposes is this technique used? What is the ball trajectory like?

Situations and Positions

- The slice lob and topspin lob are usually hit near the baseline. Sometimes a topspin lob, especially on the forehand side, is also hit between the baseline and midcourt.

Tactical Goals

- The slice lob is hit mainly in an emergency situation or when time is very short. It is a defensive move designed to gain some time (as in the shot designated *Sl* in the illustrations to the right).
- The slice lob and topspin lob are suited to playing over an opponent who is running up to the net or standing at the net. The ball should land as close as possible to the baseline, where the opponent can return it only with great difficulty, if at all. This is particularly applicable when the opponent is standing very close to the net, especially in doubles. When the ball can be hit from a solid stance and is coming in fairly slowly and not too flat (as in a weak attack by the opponent), a forehand topspin lob is the best choice. It puts a lot of speed onto the ball and sends it back into the opponent's court

very quickly after the bounce. This shot is represented by *T* in the illustrations below.

- The ball is also hit in such a way that the opponent standing at the net or running forward has great difficulty hitting a smash. This is especially the case when the ball drops steeply from a considerable height (for example, a slice lob), when the opponent can hit it only behind the body or on the backhand side, or when the trajectory of a ball with strong topspin is hard to control (topspin lob).

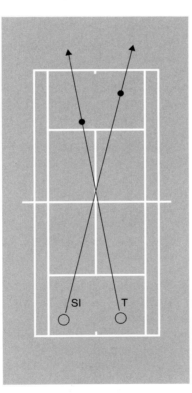

- Sometimes a topspin lob is also hit to break the opponent's rhythm or to get a momentary respite from pressure applied by the opponent.
- A slice lob can also be a response to getting lobbed over by the opponent after an attack at the net; a topspin lob can be used against a lob by an opponent who has not come forward from the baseline.

Effects on the Behavior of the Ball

- The slice lob should be hit with backspin, the topspin lob with strong topspin.
- For playing over the opponent, the ball should be hit neither too low nor too high. In the former case, the opponent must not be able to hit a smash. In the latter, the opponent must not be given enough time to run to the ball.
- For a shot designed to get the player out of a jam or that is difficult to smash—especially into the sun—the ball should be hit as high as possible.

Fig. 130   Aiming points (*left*).

Fig. 131   Ball trajectory (*below*).

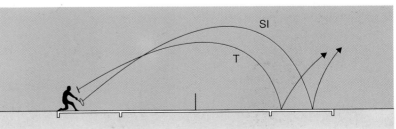

Fig. 132

Slice Lob

What does the player do in a slice lob to achieve the desired ball trajectory? What is this technique used for?

Features of the Main Action Within the Stroke Phase

- The racket is swung forward and upward with an open racket face (illustrations 5 and 6) to hit the ball with backspin into a steep trajectory.
- The ball is hit at the side and, especially with a backhand slice lob, well in front of the body with a slightly open racket face (illustration 6); this facilitates optimal energy transfer.
- Just before contact, the wrist is brought into a position that corresponds to the departure velocity to create the highest degree of accuracy.
- At contact, the grip is tightened and the wrist is held firmly for a brief instant to provide resistance to the ball.

Features of Supporting Actions

Backswing

- For a backhand slice lob, the racket is held with a backhand grip; a forehand grip is used for the forehand slice lob. This will allow you to hit the ball at a point far enough from your body to assure an efficient energy transfer.
- The backswing starts by turning the upper body rearward (farther for a backhand than for a forehand shot); the racket is brought back in a flat arc.
- In the transition to the stroke phase, the racket face is open so it will be in the right position when the ball is hit (illustrations 2–4).
- The right leg (or the left leg in a forehand slice lob), which is the support leg in the stroke and follow-through, is advanced in the direction of the anticipated shot (illustrations 1 and 2). Feet should be kept at least hip width apart to maintain balance. With a backhand slice lob, the lateral position is so pronounced that the right half of the back points to the net.

Stroke Phase

- The racket is swung forward and downward with a very open racket face.
- The support leg bends deeply at the knee (illustrations 3–6); this aids in the downward movement of the racket at the start of the stroke movement.
- The forward leg gradually straightens in conjunction with the main action directed upward.
- For a backhand slice lob, the arm is straight in the main action (illustration 4). This occurs because the racket arm is in front of the body and the elbow is sharply bent in the backswing. With a forehand slice lob, the arm is slightly bent throughout.

Follow-through

- Many players are content to hit both forehand and backhand using the *semicontinental grip*. This has no real disadvantage since the racket face does not need to be vertical at contact.
- The *length, timing, and dynamics of the backswing* can vary greatly among individuals, especially in the transition between the backswing and the stroke phase.
- The arm can be bent to varying degrees in a backhand slice lob.

Stroke Phase

- In a competitive situation, if a player wants to deceive the opponent into expecting a ground stroke, for example, then the racket face is opened *very late* in the stroke.
- If the arm was bent significantly in the backswing for a backhand slice lob, *it is straightened just before reaching the contact point.*

Follow-through

- The more forceful the stroke, the *longer and higher* the follow-through.

Common Flaws and Mistakes

Backswing

- *Little or no upper body rotation* restricts the length of the backswing. In a backhand slice lob, this makes a smooth swing impossible.
- *Excessive arm bend* in a forehand slice lob often produces a punching motion with the forearm or an excessively short stroke.
- *Little or no knee bend* means no subsequent straightening of the legs can occur in the stroke phase.

Fig. 133 Leaning back when hitting the ball.

Stroke Phase

- *Leaning back* makes it impossible to transferring the weight forward impossible and detracts from the stroke (fig. 133).
- When *the lateral stance is abandoned too early,* in other words, when the entire body rotates in conjunction with the stroke movement, shot control is diminished considerably.
- *Hitting the ball too late, too close to, or too far from the body* likewise undermines safety and control of the shot.

Follow-through

- *Ending the follow-through too early* by checking the movement has a very negative effect on ball control. In addition, too little transfer of momentum occurs, and the trajectory turns out too short.

A high follow-through after a topspin lob.

Fig. 134

Topspin Lob

What does the player do in a topspin lob to achieve the desired ball trajectory? What is this technique used for?

Features of the Main Action Within the Stroke Phase

- The racket is swung forward and steeply upward to hit the ball (illustrations 5–7) to create the steep angle of departure.
- The racket must move at a high rate of speed to give the ball the desired heavy topspin.
- The ball is hit at the side and in front of the body (between illustrations 6 and 7).
- Just before contact, the wrist is placed into a position that corresponds with the departure velocity to create the greatest degree of accuracy.

- At contact, the grip is tightened and the wrist is held firmly for a brief instant to provide resistance to the ball.

Features of Supporting Actions

Backswing
- At the start of the backswing, the racket is held with an extreme forehand grip (or backhand grip for a backhand shot) so that the racket face can be held vertically at contact and an efficient transfer of energy occurs.
- At the start of the backswing, the upper body turns to the rear (particularly with a backhand shot), and the racket is taken back (illustrations 1 and 2) to facilitate a smooth transition to the stroke phase.
- In a backhand topspin lob, the left hand guides the racket back by its throat to stabilize the backswing and help in turning the upper body to the rear.

- In a forehand topspin lob, the right leg is used as the support or anchor leg in the stroke. It is placed to the side and bears the player's weight in an open position. In a backhand topspin lob, a lateral stance is used.
- The knees bend deeply and the right leg carries the weight in a forehand and a backhand topspin lob (illustration 2).

Stroke Phase
- In the transition to the stroke phase, the racket head is brought far below the anticipated contact point (illustrations 4 and 5) so that the racket can be swung sharply upward in the stroke phase.
- In the transition between the backswing and the stroke phase of a forehand topspin lob, the explosive straightening of the legs begins. It supports the sharp upward movement where the right leg, in particular (the one closer to the hitting arm), pushes off forcefully from the court (illustrations 4–6).

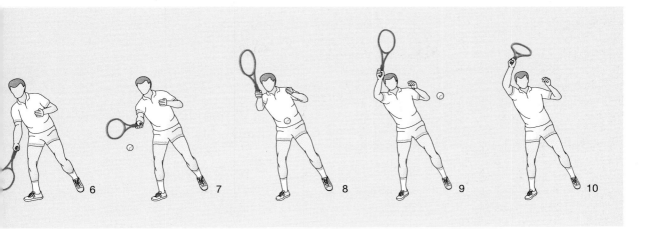

- In a forehand topspin lob, the upper body turns forward in conjunction with the stroke motion. The racket is swung upward and slightly forward in the interest of optimal energy transfer and the desired trajectory.
- In a backhand topspin lob, the body weight shifts to the forward leg. Upper body twist is minimal. The lateral position of the feet and the body is maintained up to the moment of contact to provide the best possible shot control and accuracy.
- In forehand and backhand topspin lobs, a slight backward lean occurs, especially in comparison with a normal topspin shot. This makes possible swinging the racket sharply upward even with a high contact point.

Follow-through
- The follow-through is directed sharply forward and upward (illustrations 8–10); this shows that the ball was given strong topspin.
- At the end of the follow-through, the racket is over the head (illustration 10).

Possible Variations and Their Advantages and Disadvantages

Backswing
- *The forehand or backhand grip* can vary among individuals; it corresponds to the grip used for topspin shots.
- *The length,* the height of the upper part of the loop, and the *timing and dynamics* of the backswing vary greatly among individuals, especially in the transition between taking the racket back in the backswing and moving it upward in the stroke phase.

Stroke Phase
- In the stroke phase, the backward lean can vary greatly among individual players. *A pronounced backward lean* helps in swinging the racket head vertically, especially in a backhand topspin lob.
- Upper body rotation can be exaggerated to enhance racket speed and create stronger spin.

Follow-through
- The more forceful the stroke movement, *the longer the follow-through.*
- In the follow-through, the racket can finish over the right shoulder; the racket then ends up behind the back. This is especially the case with a fairly high and late contact point.
- *When the forearm is forcefully used* in hitting the ball at an early contact point in a forehand topspin lob, the follow-through moves toward the left hip in a windshield wiper movement.

Common Flaws and Mistakes

Backswing

- *Failure to use the forehand or backhand or extreme grip variations* interferes with efficient energy transfer and creation of spin.
- *Little or no upper-body rotation* (fig. 135) restricts the length of the backswing and the eventual speed of the racket.
- *Keeping the legs too straight* likewise interferes with coordination and racket acceleration.

Stroke Phase

- *Failure to lower or raise the shoulder* (for a forehand and a backhand shot, respectively) at the start of the stroke phase detracts from setting up the main action.
- *Failure to lower the racket head* in the transition between the backswing and the stroke phase makes swinging the racket head sharply upward to the contact point impossible.
- *Straightening the legs too soon* interrupts the flow of the movement.
- *Inadequate acceleration of the racket head* results in too little topspin.
- *Hitting the ball too late or too far from or too close to the body* produces an inefficient energy transfer.

Follow-through

- *Checking the sharp upward movement* by interrupting the fluid motion is a sign that the swing was slowed before hitting the ball or was inadequate at its beginning.

Fig. 135   Too little upper-body rotation in the backswing.

Follow through
over the right shoulder
after a topspin lob.

Jump Smash

In what situations and for what purposes is this technique used? What is the ball trajectory like?

Situations and Positions

- The jump smash is usually hit in front of or behind the service line at midcourt on a very good lob by the opponent.

Tactical Goals

- A long, fairly flat lob that can be easily reached in a jump should be hit so hard that the opponent cannot get to it.
- A long and well-placed lob that can be smashed in a jump can be hit more softly, as long as it is carefully placed, in order to gain time and to set up a good ready position to launch an attack. If the ball cannot be hit as a smash, the opponent may have an opportunity to set up an attack.

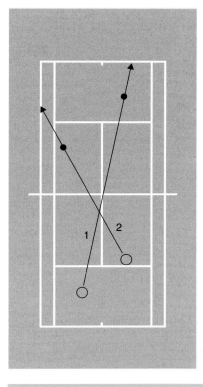

Effects on the Behavior of the Ball

- The ball may be played at high speed and with minimal spin.
- The ball may travel fairly slowly and with a little more spin.

Fig. 136 Aiming points (*left*).

Fig. 137 Ball trajectory (*below*).

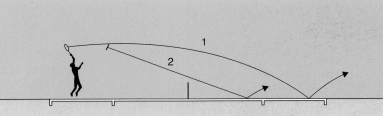

Fig. 138

Jump Smash

> What does the player do in a jump smash to achieve the desired ball trajectory? What is this technique used for?

Features of the Main Action Within the Stroke Phase

- The racket head is accelerated sharply upward and forward behind the back so it has the greatest possible speed when it hits the ball (illustrations 7–9).
- The bill is hit above or slightly in front of the head. According to the goal of the shot, the racket face is vertical or inclined slightly forward when it makes contact with the ball. This produces the desired trajectory (illustration 9).
- Due to pronation of the arm right before contact, the racket face is at a right angle to the direction of the shot (illustrations 8 and 9).

Features of the Supporting Actions

Backswing

- The racket is held with the backhand grip to create the best-possible contact point.
- At the start of the backswing, the upper body is rotated rearward (illustration 1), and the racket is brought rearward and upward in front of the right side of the body, in contrast with a serve (illustrations 2 and 3).
- Body weight shifts to the right leg, which is placed to the rear.
- To help maintain balance, the left arm is stretched high; this also complements the rearward inclination of the shoulder axis (illustrations 2 and 3).

Stroke Phase

- At the start of the stroke phase, the player jumps off the right (support) leg; the legs perform a scissors movement in the air to help with balance.
- The racket is swung at high speed through the lowest point of the loop and up to the contact point (illustrations 5–9).
- The arm continues to straighten as the wrist comes into play (illustrations 7–9).
- The upper body turns to a frontal position to support the stroke, and it leans due to the jump to the rear (illustrations 6–9).
- The ball is hit at the highest possible point (illustration 9).

8   9   10   11   12   13   14

Follow-through

- After hitting the ball, the forearm rotates less than with a service shot, and the follow-through ends in front of the left half of the body (illustration 14). Minimal pronation of the wrist to the right occurs at the end of the movement (illustrations 10 and 11).
- The player lands on the left foot. To maintain balance, the right leg points forward, and the upper body inclines slightly forward (illustration 12).
- The left arm also moves in front of the body to help maintain balance (illustrations 10 and 11).

Possible Variations and Their Advantages and Disadvantages

Backswing

- Many players hold the racket with the *semicontinental grip.*
- Many players use a pendulum motion in the backswing, as in a serve. This can lead to a delayed arm swing and time constraints in the case of fast lobs. In this case, a flattened pendulum motion should be the goal. With many players, the pendulum motion helps with the jump and leads to a more harmonious overall movement.
- *Upper body rotation can be quite pronounced,* depending on how high over the player's left shoulder the opponent's lob is played.
- *The timing of the jump can vary.* A fairly early jump permits delaying the stroke for an instant and keeping the opponent in suspense as to where the smash will be aimed.

Stroke Phase

- Many players carry out the *loop* behind the back just as far as with a serve; this can make hitting the ball accurately harder and can lead to coordination problems in a jump smash.
- *Depending on the situation, the jump is done upward or upward and rearward.*

Follow-through

- With smashes hit from far to the rear, the stroke is performed practically with the arm alone, and the *follow-through ends at chest height* with the body leaning back. This requires *a correspondingly greater scissors movement with the right leg* to help maintain balance.

Common Flaws and Mistakes

Backswing

- When *using the forehand grip*, the ball cannot be hit at the highest possible point.
- *Failure to rotate the body* interferes with proper use of the body, resulting in a slower and more tentative shot.
- *Lack of coordination between backswing and footwork* greatly reduces shot control.
- A crossover step while running backwards keeps the body facing the net.

Stroke Phase

- By *misjudging the height of the jump,* the ideal contact point cannot be achieved.

Fig. 139   Landing on the right foot (takeoff foot) after a smash.

- *Jumping too early or too late* is detrimental to coordination and control.
- *Failure to straighten the hitting arm* means the ball is hit with reduced force and below the highest possible point.
- *Hitting the ball to the side over the right shoulder* keeps the player from hitting the ball at the best-possible point.
- A *low contact point* keeps the player from hitting the ball at the best-possible point.
- *Hitting the ball too far forward* keeps the player from hitting the ball at the best-possible point.

Follow-through

- *Landing on the right foot* (fig. 139) makes a balanced landing hard after hitting the ball.
- A *short follow-through* is a sign that the ball was hit with insufficient force.

The takeoff leg (the left in this case) points to the front, and the other leg is used for the landing.

Backhand Smash

In what situations and for what purposes is this technique used? What is the ball trajectory like?

Situations and Positions
- The backhand smash is usually hit at midcourt (between the net and about 1 yard [1 m] behind the service line). It is a response to an unexpected lob volley or a lob from the opponent's midcourt that is played high over the player's backhand side, thereby making a normal smash impossible.

Tactical Goals
- The backhand smash is used despite its technical difficulties because it is effective in putting pressure onto the opponent and creating a good attack position. If the player were to let the ball bounce, that could create a difficult situation since the opponent might have an opportunity to set up an attack.

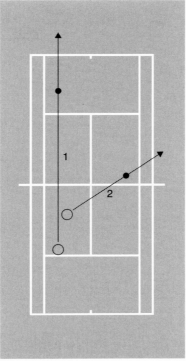

Fig. 140   Aiming points.

Fig. 141   Ball trajectory.

- The backhand smash should be played in such a way that the opponent cannot get to it or at least is put into a difficult situation. This shot is played either cross and short (as in 2) or down the line and long (1).
- A backhand smash from behind the service line should be played so that the ball lands safely and as far as possible into the opponent's court; that is the only way this shot will be effective.

Effects on the Behavior of the Ball
- The ball may be hit at a relatively high speed.
- The ball may be hit slowly and short and cross with more sidespin.

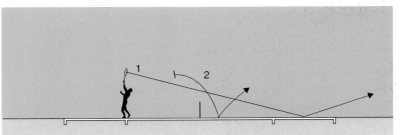

Fig. 142

Backhand Smash

What does the player do in a backhand smash to achieve the desired ball trajectory? What is this technique used for?

Features of the Main Action Within the Stroke Phase

- The racket head is accelerated in a sharply forward and upward direction (illustrations 7–9).
- At the start of the main action, the racket face is nearly at a right angle to the shot direction (illustration 9) so that the racket can be swung under control in this position right up to the contact point.
- At contact, the racket face is inclined slightly forward (illustration 10) to give the ball the desired trajectory.
- The contact point is above and slightly in front of the body (between illustrations 9 and 10).

Features of the Supporting Actions

Backswing

- The racket is held with the backhand grip to achieve the best-possible contact point.
- At the start of the backswing, the racket is brought to the rear over the backhand side; the upper body simultaneously turns to the left so that part of the back points toward the net (illustrations 1–4).
- The elbow rises so high that the racket points straight down (illustrations 5 and 6).
- The upper body leans back so that the hitting shoulder moves upward and the axis of the shoulders points sharply upward (illustrations 4–6). This is a prerequisite for hitting the ball at the desired high point in the stroke.

- Body weight is shifted onto the left (rear) leg (illustrations 1–4).
- In the second part of the backswing, the player jumps off the rear foot (illustrations 4 and 5) to achieve the highest-possible contact point.
- During the backswing, the left hand remains on the throat of the racket all the way to the lowest point of the loop to support and stabilize the backswing (illustrations 1–5).

Stroke Phase

- The arm straightens as part of a kinetic chain starting with the shoulder, then the elbow (illustrations 6–8), and finally the wrist (illustrations 9 and 10). The arm and upper body are completely extended at contact (between illustrations 9 and 10).
- The back continues to point toward the net so the arm can swing with full power.

Follow-through

- The arm continues to swing through the contact point in the direction of the shot due to the high speed of the racket head. The wrist in particular, also due to the high speed, stretches in the direction of the shot in such a way that the racket head tips sharply down (illustrations 10–12).
- The right half of the back continues pointing toward the net (illustrations 10–14).
- The left arm and the right leg are used only for maintaining balance; the player lands on the left leg.

Possible Variations and Their Advantages and Disadvantages

Backswing

- Many players hold the racket with the *semicontinental grip;* however, this grip makes getting the racket face into the best position at contact difficult.

- *At the start of the backswing,* the racket head can be taken back high and to the rear in a distinct high arc or else low and to the rear.
- After reaching the top of the arc, many players do not allow the racket head to hang straight down. However, the resulting shorter swing must be compensated for in the stroke phase either by using greater force or by using the wrist more.

Stroke Phase

- Many players hit the ball *below the highest point* and in front of the right shoulder. They do not stand under the ball, and the shot almost resembles a high backhand volley, where the angle of the racket face is rather awkward.
- Many players intentionally accelerate the racket up to the contact point in a backhand smash *with very strong wrist action;* consequently the stroke

is very fast. A prerequisite for this shot is a strong wrist.

Follow-through

- The follow-through is greatly shortened *at lower racket speeds.*
- When the ball is hit using strong wrist action, *the follow-through is shortened significantly.* The hitting arm practically remains pointing straight upward (illustrations 11–13). The follow-through is restricted by the mobility of the wrist.
- Most players land on the same leg they jump off with. However, depending on the contact point with the ball, the player may hit the ball with his or her entire back to the net. In that case, the legs cross in the air so the *player lands on the right leg* (see photo on page 168).

Common Flaws and Mistakes

Backswing
- *Inadequate rearward upper-body rotation* greatly restricts the backswing.
- *Failure to raise the elbow* over the right shoulder at the end of the backswing greatly restricts the backswing and leads to hitting the ball too low.

Stroke Phase
- If *too little momentum* is behind the stroke at the end of the backswing, the forearm is too tight, and that interferes with accelerating the racket.
- *Incomplete extension of racket arm and body* (fig. 143) means the ball is hit with reduced force and below the highest-possible point.

Fig. 143   Hitting the ball with a bent arm.

- If *rotating the upper body in the direction of the shot,* during the shot phase the racket cannot be swung to the right. This reduces the amount of force applied up to the contact point. A correction has to be made to present the racket face in the right position at contact by turning the forearm.
- *Little or no wrist action* in the main action means the racket moves too slowly and the ball cannot be hit hard enough.

Follow-through
- *Turning the upper body to face the direction of the shot* is a sign that the upper body has rotated in the stroke phase.

Service—Slice and Twist (Kick)

> In what situations and for what purposes is this technique used? What is the ball trajectory like?

In slice and twist serves, the ball is given quite a bit of topspin and sidespin in comparison with a ground shot serve (see pages 104–105). Sidespin predominates in a slice serve; with a twist serve, topspin is more usual.

Situations and Positions

- The slice and twist serves are hit from behind the baseline and depending on the score, from right or left of the center mark. Usually, this technique is used for a second serve.

Tactical Goals

- The ball is hit into the diagonally opposite service court.
- The slice or twist service is intended to place the opponent in such a difficult situation through a combination of spin, speed, and accuracy that the stage is set either for a mistake on the return or for a direct point by the server on the next hit.

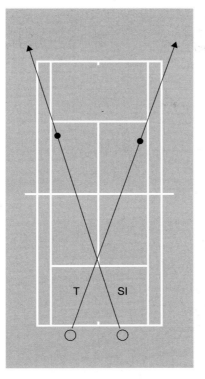

- A slice service from the right to the opponent's forehand side should be played in such a way as to force the opponent far out of the court. The effects of sidespin on a bouncing slice serve become more disconcerting to an opponent as the smoothness of the surface increases. This shot is used extensively on indoor courts.
- A twist serve is usually hit from the left side to the opponent's backhand side to drive the opponent out of the court. It also sets up a high contact point since this service bounces high. Topspin in a bounce creates difficulties for the opponent in proportion to the roughness of the court surface. More roughness accentuates the effects of the spin.

Effects on the Behavior of the Ball

- In a slice service, the ball should travel in a flat trajectory when hit with stronger sidespin than topspin.
- In a twist serve, the ball with strong topspin should cross the net in a higher and more curving arc.

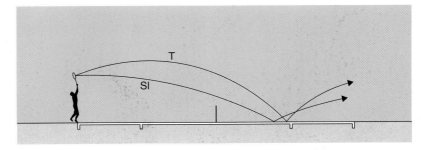

Fig. 145 Ball trajectory (*Sl* = slice; *T* = twist).

Technique

Fig. 146 Slice service.

Fig 147 Twist service.

Service—Slice and Twist (Kick)

What does the player do in a slice or twist serve (fig. 146 and 147, respectively) to achieve the desired ball trajectory? What are these techniques used for?

Features of the Main Action Within the Stroke Phase

- The racket head accelerates sharply forward and upward behind the back (illustrations 9–12) to reach optimal speed at contact.
- Depending on the type of shot (slice or twist), the racket is swung through the contact point either angling to the side (slice) or more steeply upward (twist); see illustrations 11 and 12.

- At the contact point, the racket head is practically vertical to the ground and at a right angle to the direction of the shot (illustration 12) to give the ball the desired trajectory.
- The contact point is so high that on the one hand, it facilitates weight transfer forward and upward and on the other hand, it helps in creating the desired spin. Depending on the spin combination, the ball can be hit farther to the right (with a slice) or to the left

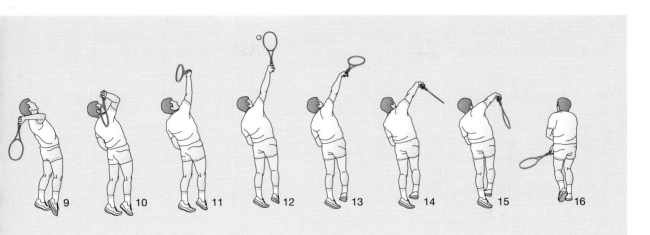

(with a twist) than with a ground shot serve (see illustration 12).

Features of Supporting Actions

Backswing
- The racket is held with the backhand grip.
- Feet are kept about shoulder width apart for a stable ready position.
- At the start of the backswing, the racket is first brought downward in a pendulum movement and then to the rear and upward (illustrations 1–4).
- At the same time, the upper body turns to the rear and the body weight momentarily shifts to the right leg (illustrations 1–4). With a slice, the upper body rotation is somewhat stronger than with a twist.
- At the start of the pendulum movement, the ball is brought upward by straightening the left arm and keeping the wrist firm (illustrations 2–4).
- The upward movement of the ball arm is roughly aligned with the right net post so the ball can be brought under control to the best contact point (illustration 4).
- The hand releases the ball at about forehead height (illustration 3); this affords good control over the height and direction of the toss.
- The ball is tossed high enough so it can be hit after it reaches its highest point.

Technique

- The axis of the shoulders inclines increasingly rearward and downward (illustrations 3–5).
- The upper body begins leaning back when the weight is transferred to the left foot (illustration 5).
- At this point the pelvis is thrust forward.
- The knees—especially the left one—bend (illustrations 5 and 6).
- The upper body leans increasingly to the rear (illustrations 6 and 7). This completes the tensioning of the bow, which generally is a bit stronger in a twist service than in a slice service. This tensioning sets up a long acceleration path and supports the desired acceleration in the main action.
- As the knees bend, the racket is brought over the right shoulder by bending the elbow (illustrations 5 and 6).

Stroke Phase
- The body is straightened from low to high at the contact point; in other words, the legs are the first to extend (illustrations 6–8).
- After that, the muscles of the hips, stomach, chest, and shoulders contract in succession (illustrations 8–10); at the end, the wrist bends (illustration 12).
- While the body straightens, the torso turns in the direction of the shot; this upper-body rotation is more pronounced in the slice service than in the twist service. In other words, in a twist, the upper body does not face the front at contact, as it does in a slice, and the body weight is distributed on the left foot.

- The racket accelerates up to the contact point.
- The dynamic straightening usually produces a jump off the left foot.
- The hitting arm is completely extended and the shoulder is as high as possible so the ball can be hit at the best possible point. At contact, the left foot, right shoulder, and racket hand align on a vertical axis (illustration 12).
- With a twist, the right foot moves rearward and to the side in the main action because of the direction of the stroke and the relatively minor upper-body rotation (illustrations 10–12).

Follow-through
- After the ball is hit, the right forearm rotates to the outside and swings to the right (illustrations 13 and 14). With a twist, the first part of the follow-through is directed more to the right than with a slice; this is due to the direction in which the racket is moving (illustrations 13 and 14).
- Because of the high rate of acceleration of the racket in the main action and the rotation of the arm at the start of the follow-through, the wrist turns forward and to the right (pronation, see illustrations 14 and 15).
- In a slice service, the upper body follows the ball in the direction of the shot (illustrations 14 and 15). In a twist service, the body at first leans a bit left, using little rotation, in the interest of

balance and coordination. Subsequently, it turns in the direction of the shot (illustrations 14 and 15).
- With both serves, the left foot contacts the court and helps with weight distribution.
- The arm swings through in front of the body in a low arc to the left side (illustration 16).

Possible Variations and Their Advantages and Disadvantages

Backswing
- Many players use the *semicontinental grip* for both of these serves. This may make creating enough spin impossible.
- Possible *variations in synchronizing the movement of the racket and the ball toss* exist:
  - Many players bring both hands downward at the same time and at the same speed and then raise them simultaneously.
  - Many players raise the ball with a fairly short, quick movement of the left hand.
  - Many players move the arms in opposite directions from the ready position: downward with the right arm and racket and upward with the left arm and ball.

All three methods can produce satisfactory serves. Depending on how the individual actions are linked together, there are certain consequences for the height of the ball toss.

- Many players forgo the pendulum movement to the rear; rather, they lift the racket beside the body. This helps them with timing and coordination.
- The ball can also be tossed up *with a slight bend in the arm.*
- The *direction of the ball toss* has variations. In a slice service, many players toss the ball farther to the right front and in a twist service, farther to the left rear. These variations enhance the effect of the corresponding spin (fig. 148). A disadvantage is that these actions signal to the opponent what type of spin to expect.
- Many players start with the *weight on the right foot.* In this case, they must take care to avoid planting the left foot too soon when the weight is transferred to the left leg.
- The right foot can *be placed forward at different distances.* The crucial points are to avoid turning the hip too early in placing the foot and making sure the foot does not touch or step over the baseline.

Fig. 148 Direction of the toss for a twist (*above*) and a slice (*below*).

Stroke Phase
- In the backswing and stroke phases, *timing and dynamics* usually vary among individual players.
- Players use different *body rotations in a slice or rearward lean in a twist service* according to the direction of the ball toss to enhance the effect of the spin. Differences also occur in how the body is used, particularly with players of large or small physical stature: larger players tend to tension the bow less.
- Players also bend the knees to different degrees, especially in a twist service.
- *Many players jump off the left* leg when playing forcefully. With a twist, this jump follows the forward direction of the shot.

Follow-through
- The more forcefully the body is used in a twist service to create the sharp upward movement of the racket, the greater the tendency to *jump up from the court* and bring the right leg *rearward and to the side* to maintain balance. Body weight is distributed on the left foot at landing.

Common Flaws and Mistakes

Backswing

- Using the *forehand grip* makes hitting the ball at the best possible point impossible.
- Frontal body position reduces the momentum that comes from rotating the body.
- *Pulling the upper arm in to the torso* by bending the elbow interferes with the flow of motion and racket acceleration.
- *Straightening the knees prematurely* means no forward and upward weight transfer can occur. This usually happens because the body weight was already distributed on the forward foot at the start of the backswing.
- *Failure to bend the knees* makes transferring movement upward impossible.
- *Not tossing the ball high enough* leads to a hasty backswing and stroke and keeps the player from hitting the ball at the best possible point.
- In a *slice service, the ball is tossed too far left or to the rear* or in a *twist service, too far right or forward.* The arm movement required to create the desired spin is almost impossible.

Stroke Phase

- *Interrupting the flow of the movement at the lowest point of the loop* interferes with using the racket with maximum force at contact.
- *Failure to straighten the racket arm* leads to hitting the ball with reduced force and below the highest-possible point.
- *Insufficient racket speed* at contact gives the ball too little velocity and spin.
- *Shifting the weight rearward to the right foot* causes the body to lean back, thereby adversely affecting the safety and accuracy of the shot. Additionally, since the body weight is too far back, the body cannot be used in the direction of the shot.
- *Straightening the arm too early* (long before making contact) greatly interferes with acceleration.
- *Advancing the right foot too early in the direction of the shot* produces premature body rotation.
- *Drawing the pelvis back* results from a premature straightening of the body; the ball cannot be hit at the best-possible point.

Follow-through

- *Swinging through with the racket arm* very fast to the left (especially with a slice) and advancing the right leg too soon in a twist serve greatly reduce shot control.

Individualized Technique in Championship Tennis

A careful analysis of world-class players who have achieved a high degree of perfection in stroke technique in the face of tremendously difficult demands shows that in championship tennis, technique is marked by some highly individualized traits. However, at the same time, it largely conforms with the basics described in this book.

Thus, assuming that those top-level techniques are based on different rules or principles from the techniques of the average player would be erroneous. Top-level competitors had to pass through various stages in their years of playing as they progressed from the basics described in this book to their very accomplished and individualized techniques. They are able to apply their tactical goals in especially difficult situations because of their individualized style and their strict adherence to the basic principles of technique. They are especially able to combine fast running, high-speed shots, superb accuracy, and economy of movement.

This is what allows them to focus on the essentials. An observer might get the impression that the techniques of champions and of average players differ greatly.

Top-level players function mainly *at higher speeds* than average players. Just the same, they play with *great reliability and accuracy.*

High speed in baseline shots is achieved largely in accordance with biomechanical principles. Thus, top-level players use considerably more pronounced and stronger *body rotation;* in addition, they push off quite hard from the court surface. They therefore rotate the right shoulder and hip (for right-handed players) in the direction of the shot and jump upward. The rotation radius of the shoulder axis can exceed 200 degrees.

Top-level players also make good use of upper-body rotation in the backhand. As a result, the direction of the follow-through is parallel to the baseline or even above it.

Top-level players have developed outstanding coordination. Therefore, they can transfer force as effectively as possible even in difficult situations and using abbreviated strokes.

They increasingly prefer the open stroke position since it affords better tensing of the mus-cles involved and saves needed energy and time. This is true not only for the forehand (which predominates at all levels of play down to and including the youngest players) but also for the backhand, especially the two-handed backhand.

Top-level players also make *maximum use of the wrist;* it helps them accelerate the racket to the maximum without expending extra energy. This is particularly important in the abbreviated strokes in the difficult situations just mentioned.

With quite a number of top-level players, *the grip* varies significantly; the choice may not be appropriate or advantageous for beginners or even advanced players. This is due, in part, to a competitor's style of play, very strong forearm muscles, and the ability to improvise and adapt. *The ability to improvise* becomes evident among great players in particularly difficult situations, which even contribute to the development of certain artistic abilities. In such situations, these players condense perfect balance for a shot into a minimal time span (including the instant of the hit). Often, they are forced to hit the ball accurately while their body is moving at high speed, in the middle of a great leap, or in very awkward positions.

Index